This book is well written and full of useful information. The heart and soul of this book is drafting the vision statement. In organizations such as Burlington Northern, enlightened leadership is quite contagious.

Neil Beck
Quality Coordinator, Pacific Division
Burlington Northern Railroad

There are many books that expound on the importance of vision, leadership, and teamwork. But this book goes beyond that. It's a "how to cook" book that gets to the crux of the problem; how to get the entire organization to buy in and execute the leader's vision. The process they define, adapted to the situation and applied repetitively, will in fact greatly improve buy-in and execution.

Richard W. Brandt
Vice Chairman
Security Pacific Bank Washington

What is missing in many companies is knowing how to set direction from the top and work through the implementation. *The Visionary Leader* is an exciting book because it establishes a step-by-step process for making vision part of the fabric of an organization. Unless you have developed your culture in this way, the quality revolution will not happen in your company.

John Graham
Quality Assurance Manager
Digital Systems International, Inc.

The Visionary Leader can help all of our companies in the American Electronics Association meet the challenges of a rapidly changing environment. It provides a foundation that makes strategic planning easier.

J. Richard Iverson
President and CEO
American Electronics Association

The Visionary Leader is a powerful handbook for the Human Resource executive who is called upon to be a strategic partner with top leaders in their organization. This is an excellent tool in leading the organization through adaptive change for this decade and the next.

Pamela Taylor
Vice President, Human Resources
MetLife Capital Corporation

THE VISIONARY LEADER

THE VISIONARY LEADER
FROM MISSION STATEMENT TO A THRIVING ORGANIZATION, HERE'S YOUR BLUEPRINT FOR BUILDING AN INSPIRED, COHESIVE CUSTOMER-ORIENTED TEAM

Bob Wall, Robert S. Solum,
& Mark R. Sobol

Prima Publishing
P.O. Box 1260SOL
Rocklin, CA 95677
(916) 786-0426

Production by Carol Dondrea, Bookman Productions
Copy Editing by Anne Montague
Composition by Janet Hansen, Alphatype
Interior design by Judith Levinson
Jacket by Kirschner-Caroff Design

Prima Publishing
Rocklin, CA

Continuous Cultural Improvement™ is an organizational improvement process developed by Vision In Action, Inc.
Continuous Cultural Improvement™ is a registered trademark owned by Vision In Action, Inc.

Library of Congress Cataloging-in-Publication Data

Wall, Bob (Bob Lee)
    The visionary leader : from mission statement to a thriving organization, here's your blueprint for building an inspired, cohesive customer-oriented team/ by Bob Wall, Robert Solum, and Mark Sobol.
      p. cm.
    Includes index.
    ISBN 1-55958-163-8
    1. Leadership. I. Solum, Robert. II. Sobol, Mark.
    III. Title.
HD57.7.W34   1992
658.4'092—dc20   91-39330
                                      CIP

93 94 95 RRD   10 9 8 7 6 5 4 3 2
Printed in the United States of America

Dedicated to
Peggy, Colby, Christopher,
Matthew, Aimee, and
Marian (Tex)

The old hierarchy is ending. Your company's future depends upon leadership, trust, and participation. The only way to build them is through vision. Welcome to *The Visionary Leader.*

Robert S. Solum
Mark R. Sobol
Bob Wall

CONTENTS

ACKNOWLEDGMENTS

To our clients over the past fifteen years. This book is a summary of what we have learned together. Their leadership, courage, and heart have inspired and guided us throughout the creation of this book.

To Natasha Kern for believing in us and this book from the very start.

To Star Hamilton, Bob Rosinsky, and Peggy Solum for their tireless support, editing, and suggestions to the manuscript.

To Duane Newcomb for helping with the proposal that got this project off the ground.

To Ben Dominitz and the staff at Prima for their patience, support, and sage advice.

To James Bavendam, Ph.D., for his talent and wisdom in having surveys show us the truth about organizations, and for his contributions to Chapter 12.

To our associates at Vision In Action, Star Hamilton, James Bavendam, Randall Benson, John Zoulas, and Constance Durham, for helping us to expand what is possible.

To colleagues of Bob Wall and Associates, Barry Wolborsky, John Ross, and Jack Benedict, for their unflagging support throughout this project.

A Special Thanks to Our Editor, Michael Bowker

Michael's help on this book went far beyond his work as our chief editor. From the beginning, he understood and enthusiastically shared our vision of the new organization. During the year it took us to write this book, Michael guided its formation with consummate skill. His hand can be seen in the easy flow of the book and in the clarity of its message.

Michael is an author in his own right, having written "Playing From the Heart" (Prima Publishing, 1990), among other books. He is also a nationally published newspaper and magazine writer. Michael lives in Placerville, California.

UNDERSTANDING THE CHANGE

1

THE NEW
ORGANIZATION

There are more than a few books out there predicting that dramatic changes lie ahead for savvy American and international business leaders. This book is not one of them. We believe the change is already here.

Challenged by increased competition and consumer quality demands, and a growing scarcity of qualified employees, business leaders are faced with a choice, right now: either rebuild their organizations to seize the new opportunities that are presenting themselves, or be left behind.

At the heart of this reorganization is the dismantling of the outdated, top-down authority structure that defines so many of America's struggling corporations. In its place, a new concept of organization is being developed, one that spurs creativity, empowers employees, encourages learning, and ensures customer satisfaction. It is a streamlined organization—stripped of middle-management bureaucracy—with a free flow of communication throughout its horizontal form.

The ultimate structures of the new organization are still being determined. Prototypes are being developed around self-managed work teams, networks of flexible task groups, quality improvement teams, and other concepts. Which structures will withstand the test of time is still a matter of speculation. In all probability, several will emerge as winners.

In the meantime, a certain amount of confusion is being created by the reorganization. The company's mission and the employees' roles are being redefined, putting the pressure squarely on the company leaders to keep the whole thing together.

It is precisely during these times of chaos that leaders must possess one property: the ability to develop and share a clearly defined sense of direction—a vision of the desired future.

The strength of a leader's vision, and his or her ability to articulate that vision to employees, will be the measure of leadership in the 21st-century organization.

This book is designed to help you define and implement a corporate vision that can be your competitive edge in today's challenging and changing business environment. It lays out the practical steps to help you carry that vision to the front lines of your organization. Equally important, we will provide leadership tools to build the trust and participation necessary to make your vision a reality.

There is very little "theory" in this book. We've tried to stick with what we know best: the practical side of what actually works and what doesn't in the marketplace. We designed this book to help you blow the doors off your slower-moving competition by creating the best work environment your employees ever had.

But before we get to the hands-on chapters, we wanted to provide some background about why the new leadership is needed. These first two chapters take a quick, hard look at the economic and sociological changes that are redefining the role of America's business leaders. At the heart of these changes is the recognition that in order to compete in a worldwide market, American companies must set a quality goal of meeting their customers' expectations 100 percent of the time while making zero mistakes and generating zero waste. While this may be an unachievable goal, it is an enormously powerful vision. Leaders must harness the remarkable force of that vision if they hope to succeed in today's global economy.

DEMING AND JAPAN

Until recently, few Americans had ever heard of management expert W. Edwards Deming. Those who haven't are still likely to believe that the reasons Japan is successfully competing against the United States in the world market are cheap labor, the extraordinary Japanese work ethic, or a nonrestrictive government. Although these assumptions remain prevalent among American businesspeople, they are false.

Japanese industrialists are continually surprised at these American misconceptions. They are the first to say that the major reason for their successes is their adherence to the concepts espoused by an American—Deming—whose ideas fell on deaf ears when he introduced them here in the late 1940s.

Deming, along with Joseph Juran and other quality pioneers, helped introduce new methods of quality assurance in U.S. industry during World War II. At the heart of his concepts is an investigation into the causes of poor quality. They asked a simple question: Any time a business fails to achieve 100 percent customer satisfaction or zero mistakes, what is the cause? Juran's studies showed, contrary to traditional thinking, that 85 percent of poor quality was a result of poor work systems, and only 15 percent was attributable to worker error.

The ramifications of those studies—and the subsequent body of research that has ratified Juran's work—are enormous. When you accept the findings, it becomes clear that to achieve 100 percent customer satisfaction with zero mistakes, work systems must be improved. The question then becomes: Who knows the most about those systems? The answer is simple: The employees, the front line, those who work with these systems daily, those who deal directly with the customers or the product know the most about them and thus know where improvements should be made. Yet in most American businesses, who has the sole authority to make these changes? Management. In most organizations it is the managers, many of them separated from the product or customer by several layers of bureaucracy, who still make 100 percent of those decisions.

It is an approach that has failed.

The inherent problem is obvious. *In traditional organizations, the authority to examine and make improvements in the work methods is in the wrong hands—management's. Any company driven by a vision of 100 percent customer satisfaction with zero defects must be willing to relocate that authority from management to the front lines.*

Seizing on Juran's work, Deming took the bold stance that managers should acknowledge that they need employees not only to do the work, but to help improve the work system. He argued that managers should see their jobs as providing a continuity of purpose—a vision—while empowering frontline employees with decision-making ability. He further shocked and alienated American industrialists by saying that while making a profit was necessary, it wasn't the organization's entire reason for being. That, he said, was to provide the best product at the cheapest cost to the buyer while building a safe and inspiring work environment for the employees.

His ideas ran headlong into a unique postwar economy, however. The unsaturated American market was hungry for any goods and services available, regardless of quality. Deming's concepts were ignored because American industry was the strongest in the world, with a seemingly limitless horizon and no competitors in sight. The old top-down structure was working fine. Few saw reason to change.

Frustrated, Deming went to Japan, which was struggling to emerge from the devastation of the war. Typically brash, Deming sent invitations to 45 of Japan's top industrialists to attend his seminar. To his surprise, they all showed up. Within six weeks of implementing his concepts—which they did to save face, having attended the meeting—some of them reported productivity gains of more than 30 percent, with no capital outlays for new equipment.

These astonishing productivity gains came *from the workers themselves,* **a fact that set the pattern for Japanese industry. Today in America we are trying to catch up.**

It became abundantly clear over the next decade that Deming's way worked. The Japanese labor force, now consulted, empowered, and inspired, had become the most proficient on earth. An example of how the system succeeds can be seen in the auto industry. The average Japanese autoworker provides management with 28 suggestions yearly, and 80 percent of those suggestions are implemented. In America, only 1 out of every 37 autoworkers even provides a suggestion, and only 25 percent are implemented. That means Japanese autoworkers are 4,400 times more likely to improve their systems and procedures each year compared to U.S. workers in similar jobs. Obviously, Japanese workers are not 4,400 times smarter than their U.S. counterparts—the difference is in the organizational philosophies.

The Japanese have made Deming a national hero. The annual Deming Prize is the most highly regarded industrial award in Japan today. The award ceremony is covered on national television, and winning the prize brings national honor to the company. Monuments to Deming have been erected around the country, and he is celebrated with parades and ceremonies. On the walls of Toyota headquarters hang three pictures in a place of honor. One is of the company's founder and one is of the current chairman. But Deming's is the biggest of all.

The elevated quality of the Japanese products caught American companies flat-footed. One story that points up this fact involves an American company that in 1983 was negotiating to buy products from a Japanese manufacturer. The company was IBM, who had established what they believed were rigid standards for quality. "We will accept no more than three defects per ten thousand units—can you do business on those terms?" asked IBM. The Japanese manufacturer assured them that they could meet the requirement. When IBM received the order a few weeks later, it was accompanied by a cover letter that said: "We have a difficult time understanding how you do business, but we have enclosed your defective parts under separate cover."

A few years ago—some 40 years after he first began talking about the need to reorganize the way we do business—Deming was "discovered" by U.S. executives. He has since worked with dozens of the top industries in the country. His biggest success came in the mid-1980s with the Ford Motor Company. Upon instituting his concepts, Ford surged from near bankruptcy in 1980 to outearning General Motors in 1986. It was the first time in 62 years that Ford surpassed GM. Said Ford president Don Peterson, "We owe the turnaround to our commitment to the adoption of the methods of W. Edwards Deming."

Our purpose in providing this background on Deming isn't to deify him or the Japanese methods—although it is clearly the success story of this half of the century. Rather, we wanted to show why so many U.S. companies are now struggling in the fight of their lives—the fight to produce quality products at a low cost. Though the Japanese and an increasing number of U.S. companies have proven that these two ideas, quality and low cost, are not mutually exclusive, others have not yet gotten the message. Those companies, still laboring under their traditional top-down hierarchies, will not survive the competition.

THE QUALITY REVOLUTION

In 1978, only 30 percent of the respondents in a U.S. consumer poll said they considered quality more important than price when purchasing a product or service.

A similar poll taken in 1990 showed a dramatic shift in attitudes among American consumers. More than 70 percent now said that quality was the more important consideration. The shift reflects an increased awareness among buyers that quality products last longer, work better, and in the long run are more economical than cheap ones. Even products positioned at the low end of the markets are not exempt from consumers' heightened expectations.

This quality revolution began in Japan, where one of the primary commandments became "Do it right the first time." Meanwhile, American companies were still following the old line of Sears & Roebuck, where quality control meant always cheerfully replacing defective products free of charge. As a result of their commitment to quality, the average Japanese company is now only required to spend less than 10 percent of their operating budget on finding and fixing mistakes. In comparison, American companies still spend an average of 25 percent of their operating budget fixing mistakes.

By empowering frontline employees to make design suggestions and decisions, the Japanese have been able to greatly improve their production processes and ultimately the quality of their products. Perhaps the best example comes from Japanese automakers. Thanks to better-designed and higher-quality parts, only half as many worker hours are needed to produce a car in Japanese plants as compared to their American counterparts.

It is a stunning advantage that has enabled Japan to compete successfully worldwide. In the past 20 years, Japan's share of the American auto market has grown from 0.22 percent to more than 25 percent; American color television manufacturers have shrunk from 25 companies to zero; and the entire consumer electronics market is owned by the Japanese. The American businesses in these markets have virtually disappeared or been forced to change.

The new reality is that to survive the next decade, American companies must perform substantially better, devoted to a standard of zero defects and 100 percent customer satisfaction. Today, all American businesses must join that revolution or forever be reactive to their competition. But companies cannot approach this ideal without an inspired work force. If the workers are not committed to quality and to improving the system, companies will continue to spend a quarter of their budget on fixing mistakes.

Exhorting workers to do their best isn't the answer. They are already doing their best. What is needed instead is a constant improvement of design and the production process. For that to happen, managers must have the full involvement and support of the frontline workers.

Take This Job and Love It!

For business leaders, the baby boom has gone bust. National demographics show a dramatic drop in the number of workers entering the marketplace in the next decade. Expanded technical skills are now required of most employees, while at the same time, education levels are declining throughout the country. Frustrated by layers of bureaucracy and rigid top-down authority structures, workers are losing their company loyalty. As a result, it is becoming increasingly difficult to find qualified workers and even more difficult to keep them.

Finding and keeping skilled employees will become one of the make-or-break factors for American businesses over the next 20 years. The current statistics on employee retention are not encouraging, and they are likely to grow worse as skilled employees become a more valued commodity and competition for them increases. The average American worker now stays with a company less than three years before moving on. In the Silicon Valley in California, young professionals are referred to as "walking floppy disks," because they stay with a company just long enough to develop new skills and learn how the company works. Then they are off to the next position, taking everything they know with them.

Obviously this is expensive for organizations, which are forced to invest large sums recruiting and training. But the solution to securing worker loyalty isn't to pay higher and higher salaries. As a visionary leader, your goal is to encourage employees to accept personal ownership of the company's mission. It is to build the type of cultural values and participative environment inside your organization that will attract them and keep them challenged and motivated.

SOME PROFITABLE REORGANIZATIONS

So far, we've discussed some of the major factors that are forcing American businesses to change the way they are organized. But just *how* are successful businesses being reorganized?

The elimination of the old top-down management style—the dismantling of the authoritarian hierarchy—is the first step toward future success. One of the best examples comes out of Park City, Utah, headquarters of Mrs. Fields Cookies, Inc., the world's largest retailer of cookies and specialty bakery products. In the past decade, the company's gross sales have skyrocketed from $25 million to $200 million. Randy Fields, chairman of the company (his wife Debbi is president and chief executive officer), says one of the chief reasons for the big payoff has been the flattening of the organizational chart. By utilizing computers, voice mail, and other information technologies, Fields has managed to virtually eliminate middle management and push decision making out to the front lines—the retailers themselves, who are closest to the customer.

"If I'd increased corporate personnel proportionate to retail, I'd have 300 people here, not 115," Fields said.

Mrs. Fields's organizational chart is now 20 times wider than it is high. The company is hardly alone in its strategy. Such mainstream companies as Levi Strauss, AT&T, General Electric, Ford, Xerox, GM, IBM, Honeywell, Delta Air Lines, Boeing, Motorola, and Du Pont have begun moving toward a breaking down of the old structures.

Tom Peters labeled this dismantling of the top-down hierarchy "Revolution 2000"—the greatest change in the way we organize work since the beginning of the industrial revolution.

Rather than an organizational chart endlessly layered like an onion, "Revolution 2000," in a broad sense, calls for groups of self-managed work teams, each responsible for carrying out projects from start to finish. With few horizontal barriers, these work teams report directly to top management. The teams work in a self-directed manner. They are closer to the customer than the insulated middle management layers and can better translate customer needs and desires into viable products and services. Utilizing the best computer technology, they have the latest information at their fingertips and have the authority to make their own decisions.

PEOPLE ARE THE PRIORITY

"GE's moves bear the twin hallmarks of the new-paradigm thinking: the systems view—seeing everything as interconnected—and the focus on people," wrote *Fortune* magazine reporter Frank Rose. Companies are also beginning to pay close attention to internal corporate culture. They have realized that making the work environment a friendlier place pays big dividends.

One of the better examples of this thinking is the startling changes that have occurred in the United Services Automobile Association, the 13,000-employee insurance giant. The company has made a 100 percent commitment to creating a work environment that is the best any of its employees have ever had. The corporate headquarters in San Antonio is brightly landscaped, but it is internally where the organization really shines. Employees on work teams are encouraged to submit ideas, which are recognized and celebrated. Health and social issues are continually addressed through free seminars and a team of on-staff professional counselors, and the company spends $19 million (2.7 percent of its budget) on career training. In 1991, about 1,800 employees were enrolled in college courses given in 60 classrooms on the premises by area colleges. Those going on to graduate work have their tuition paid, including fees for CPA exams. USAA also boasts a four-day, 39-hour workweek and a fleet of 150 vans that offer employees a subsidized daily commute.

There are those in the corporation who have cried "Enough!" but their protests have been buried in an avalanche of astonishing results. Since instituting this program, USAA, once invisible in the rankings, has become the fifth-largest automobile insurance company, the sixth-largest in homeowners' policies, and it has branched into banking, real estate, financial management, travel service, and life insurance. It has expanded its owned and managed assets from $200 million to $19 billion.

At the heart of these advances is the company's success in dealing with its people. Last year it received 34,970 applications for 1,248 jobs. The turnover rate in the company was an industry-low 7 percent in 1990, and the absenteeism rate was below 2 percent.

Robert McDermott, chief executive officer for USAA, has based the company-wide change on one overriding visionary principle. "We try to treat our people the way we want them to treat the customers."

Other companies are making similar moves.

- At a Levi Strauss factory in Fayetteville, Arkansas, employees cure boredom and boost productivity by learning one another's jobs. They formed teams and decided for themselves how the work was to be done. The process, which was proposed from the factory floor, has been an overwhelming success and is being exported to other factories.

- To promote a feeling of participation among its 10,000 employees, Wang Laboratories has instituted an open-door policy allowing any employee to attend any company meeting.

- General Motors has more than 100 staff psychologists available to help with problems involving job burnout, family crises, divorces, conflict resolution methods, drugs, and alcohol.

- IBM, Motorola, Corning Glass, Pepsico, Xerox, and other companies, worried about turnover and absenteeism, are instituting a variety of programs to enhance the work environment. These include everything from multilevel task forces for identifying and solving problems to day-care centers.

- A number of smaller companies are also utilizing some creative approaches. The owner of a roofing company near Seattle told us that he was having difficulty keeping his crew "out of the doughnut shops and on the roofs where they belonged." They also showed little desire to help maintain his equipment, which cost him dearly in downtime. Frustrated, he decided to try an innovative approach. He stopped paying his crew by the hour and instead gave them 30 percent of each job they did. They were allowed to create any work method they wanted; however, if they made errors and had to do a roof over again, they did so on their own time. Given this kind of authority and motivation, his crew quickly became the best in the area. Although he paid his employees a higher percent of each job, their vastly higher efficiency rate increased everybody's income by more than 50 percent from the year before.

These changes result from a recognition of demographic shifts. Those entering the work force are no longer satisfied with a simple job description under a rigid authoritarian system. They demand to have more of a say in decisions that affect them. They want and expect more freedom and independence. In return, they will work for the company at accelerated levels of creativity and productivity.

It is the greatest bargain American businesses have ever been offered.

However, as encouraging as these changes are, *they are just the beginning!* Merely improving employee conditions, important as this is, isn't enough. In order to fully implement these changes and make them permanent, companies must go further—much further.

CAPTURING HEARTS AND MINDS

The idea that workers should be rewarded in the soul as well as the pocketbook is no longer dismissed as a notion thought up in some California hot tub. Increasingly, a new consciousness is coming of age in the more progressive companies, one that focuses on people, not machinery or organizations. Leaders like Robert Haas of Levi Strauss have altered their organizations so that managers are no longer looked upon as authority figures, but rather as role models, educators, and facilitators. Employees are given the best training possible and encouraged to understand and share in the mission of the organization and make it their own. They are empowered to make decisions and turned loose to reach their fullest potential.

The result has been that companies which have reformed their vertical structures have saved an average of 20 percent in reduced costs resulting from improved work methods and innovations. More important to the long-term health of the organizations is that these challenging work environments act as a magnet that attracts and holds on to spirited employees, who are more motivated and committed.

The new leaders understand one crucial fact: that personal fulfillment and business success cannot be separated. "Productivity is the key," said General Electric's head of management development, James Baughman. "You can only get so much more productivity out of reorganization and automation. Where you really get productivity leaps is in the minds and hearts of people."

A TYRANNOSAURUS, BUT STILL A DINOSAUR

Perhaps the hardest part for most business leaders in retooling their organizational structure is letting go of old ideas. After all, the old paradigm—the Newtonian, linear, mechanistic view, which was fully realized by Henry Ford and his assembly-line approach—has been around since before most of us were born. The top-down hierarchy was refined into its present form by Frederick Winslow Taylor, Ford's organizational consultant.

At the time, the structure made sense. Taylor was faced with a largely immigrant work force. Most of the employees were uneducated and many spoke no English. To overcome those problems, Taylor devised a division of labor whereby each worker would be assigned and trained to do just one thing—over and over again. It solved the communication gap. As long as each worker did his assigned task, the entire system added up to the production of a new automobile.

The final product was the domain of the *boss,* whose job was to ensure that all the individual pieces of the job fit together. Because his point of view was of the entire product, his vantage point was "higher" than that of the employees. They were not required to understand the big picture; in fact, they were discouraged from trying. Any departure from the rigidly structured system, and the entire latticework of steps would fall apart; therefore, the style of the managers was usually heavy-handed.

The Taylor hierarchy is the legacy that was left us by our parents and grandparents. It is what we understood, if only subconsciously, as we grew up about how the world around us worked. It is the view that we were taught to revere and respect. Its ultraconservative structure was based on absolute and unquestioned order, starting from the top down. At its best, it was a powerful force, a tyrannosaurus among the dinosaurs. The problem, of course, is that it is still a dinosaur, out of place and pace in today's environment.

I'M OK, YOU'RE OK (BUT I'M STILL THE BOSS)

Following World War II, experts in Great Britain and the United States began to study group dynamics in the work force. Consultants at London's Tavistock Institute started encouraging business leaders to give their technical workers greater responsibility in factories and coal mines. In America, thinkers at the Massachusetts Institute of Technology were developing a new theory based on sensitivity training—the T-group—which championed the personal growth of the worker. The notion grew slowly throughout the 1950s and '60s, fueled in part by psychologist Abraham Maslow's idea that the managers in the best companies strove toward the self-actualization of their employees. The approach was based on an improved quality of life for the workers and concerned itself only incidentally with the quality of the product.

The human potential movement suddenly shifted into high gear in the 1970s, as we began to look inward to heal the psychic wounds left by Vietnam and the turbulent 1960s. Books like *I'm OK, You're OK* hit the best-seller list, and personal-growth advocates suddenly gained credibility by grabbing huge consulting contracts from companies like TRW and Ford. One of the first things these consultants did was to enlarge the role of the leader. Management was seen as requiring more skill than had been previously recognized. Not only did the manager have to possess technical skills, he or she now had to display interpersonal skills as well. For the first time, leaders were expected not only to command, but also to listen. Workshops, such as Leadership Effectiveness Training, were required of most managers, who were taught to encourage communication with employees, and to resolve conflicts.

By the end of the 1970s, management training had become a big business, but in the final assessment, the effort largely failed.

The aim of the human potential movement was a good one, but it was doomed before it started. It stressed the values of participation and personal growth, but did nothing to change the structure of the top-down hierarchy. Employees were taught to think for themselves and act independently, yet they were stifled by the same layers of bureaucracy that created the need for a human potential movement in the first place. In many cases, the hypocrisy cost management its credibility.

THE NEW VISION

The human potential movement did accomplish one important thing, however. It helped nurture the belief in the baby boom generation that personal fulfillment is a birthright. It raised expectations that the workplace could be a creative, fulfilling arena, and therefore the movement was a necessary forerunner to the changes now under way.

Yet the new paradigm—the new vision—that is emerging is more practical than altruistic. Authority is being shifted to frontline workers not to help them actualize themselves but to improve quality and productivity. At the heart of the new vision is one simple fact: The top-down style of making decisions is too sluggish and too removed from the action to produce the quality goods needed to compete in today's market.

At the same time, the new vision *is* based on communication, the free flow of ideas, and the reaching of full human potential. It puts people—the employees and the customers—first. In the new view, rigid organizational lines give way to flexible networks, and the questioning of old thinking is not only encouraged, it's expected. The new vision is based, in part, on our recent realization that everything in our environment is interconnected. No longer can you separate a person from his or her work.

Although it emerged as a direct response to increased foreign and domestic competition, the new vision has found perhaps an even more important application in its approach to the two principal human challenges: customer satisfaction and employee productivity.

The new vision requires a dramatic letting go of the conventional values that ossified around the old top-down hierarchy. It will demand far more leadership qualities than
ever before. It calls for full and daily communication between managers and workers in a work culture that fosters trust, learning, participation, and dignity, and it
depends on leaders who are committed to it.

As altruistic as this new view might seem, it is soundly
based in and ultimately driven by its practical applications.
Frankly, there is no other route to the promised land of
high-quality, low-priced products.

2

THE LEADER'S NEW ROLE

No plan or vision, regardless of the cleverness or quality of its design, will work without enlightened leadership to carry it out. This is especially true as organizations begin to dismantle the old command and control structures. The new leader has two primary roles. One is to have a vision and implement it. The other is to prepare people in the company to assume greater responsibility. First, of course, the leader must have a vision. This may seem an obvious step, but we have been amazed during our conversations with business leaders across the country at how many of them have not yet developed a strong vision. And if they do have a vision, they may lack the necessary strategies for making it a reality.

In many cases, the problem isn't that these leaders lack the ability to grasp these ideas. It is that they are afraid to "let go of the mules." This concept comes from the apocryphal story of an old Army sergeant who was serving out the last part of his career in the early part of this century. He had been a mule skinner all his life, caring for the animals that pulled the Army's cannons. Just prior to his retirement, the Army began using motorized vehicles to pull the cannons instead of mules. During target practice, however, the ancient sergeant would continue to stand behind the cannons with his arms outstretched.

"What's he doing?" asked a young soldier.

"He's still holding on to the mules," came the reply.

Though some managers may not be able to let go of old habits, for others the unwillingness to change goes even deeper. These managers, in the long run, will be the biggest obstacles to the new leader's vision. They are going to resist change at all costs either because it doesn't occur to them that they need to change or they believe the false notion that the change will force them to relinquish their personal power. The old structure has provided them with a direct span of control that they are comfortable with. Giving up that power is difficult, especially for those who lack an understanding of the new vision. These recalcitrant managers have grown up with the idea of the top-down autocracy, and now that they have reached the top, they are loath to let go of their control. In taking such a stance, however, they are jeopardizing the long-term financial health of the company and perhaps their own jobs. Out of fear, they are blowing the opportunity of a lifetime to grasp perhaps the most satisfying and profitable power of all: the chance to help others empower themselves.

UNDERSTANDING THE ROLE

In the past, managers have been technical experts who defined the jobs of their employees. In many cases, they literally wrote out job descriptions for them. In doing so, these managers asked their employees to park their brains at the door. Most of the time, the employees had no idea how their efforts fit into the bigger picture. The manager's job was to peer over the employees' shoulders to ensure they were accomplishing their work according to the specifications they were given. Hoarding information gave these managers power, but also crippled the company's ability to respond to market changes.

The role of the new leader is dramatically different. Although he or she must still be a technical expert, providing direction and developing a work environment that is free from fear and allows employees to freely express and implement their ideas are more important.

To borrow an analogy from Peter Drucker, the traditional company rests primarily on command authority, much like the military. The new company is more analogous to a symphony, where all the sections—strings, woodwinds, brass, percussion—understand their interwoven roles, but none has authority over the other. Other than the leader, the conductor, there are no "bosses" in the symphony—even the concertmaster doesn't manage the other violinists—yet they all must blend their efforts to produce just the right sound.

The new leader's role is much like a symphony conductor's: ensuring that all the autonomous sections blend together harmoniously toward a single goal.

The first person the new leader must be able to convert to his or her vision is himself. If he isn't sold on the company's mission, values, and guiding principles, it will be next to impossible for him to effectively convert his employees.

New leaders must be acutely aware of their own strengths and weaknesses. One of the biggest problems we've seen in executives we've worked with is that many are blind to themselves. They don't recognize the weaknesses they may have, especially when it comes to communicating with their employees. A leader with poor communication skills may have been able to survive in the top-down hierarchies of the past, but he or she will be an organizational albatross in the future.

New leaders' success will also hinge largely on their ability to motivate and empower other people. They must know themselves thoroughly and see themselves as an instrument of change. They must understand that *how* and *who* they are is as important as what they know. They must realize that their approach and leadership style will ultimately affect productivity as much as or more than their technical expertise.

GRASPING THE VISION

At the heart of the new paradigm—achieving maximum speed and quality through relocating authority—lies the vision of the new leader. This vision includes the broader sense of mission: who we are, why we are doing this work, why it's important, the promises we've made to the customer, and the code of conduct governing how we operate with each other. Beyond that, it also includes a more detailed discussion that evolves as a strategic plan. The plan is essential, for in the middle of the chaos that the reorganization will bring, the plan is often all there will be to hold the company together.

Understanding the vision, though, isn't enough. The new leader must be able to inspire others with the vision so that others want to say yes to it. In articulating the broader sense of mission, the new leader must be able to touch the hearts of the employees.

A survey in *Psychology Today* magazine indicated that more than 90 percent of the American workers surveyed said they want to produce the highest-quality work possible. However, more than 50 percent also said they only work hard enough to keep their jobs. The reason they had stopped trying was that they were frustrated by the obstacles the organization placed in their way. The old top-down method of management fosters layers of bureaucracy that deaden motivation. The old style of management also often uses fear as a motivator. It robs employees of their state of natural inspiration and quashes their spirits.

The new vision takes a radically different view of human nature. It recognizes that most people have tremendous levels of enthusiasm and energy and naturally want to contribute to something they feel is important. To tap that incredible energy, management must give people the authority to eliminate the obstacles they face. The new leader must be able to persuade them to invest wholeheartedly in the company's mission, through his or her vision and actions.

The Culture Builder

Removing obstacles within the workplace—especially fear—is what building an organizational culture is all about. The culture we're referring to here is the quality of the relationships that exist between people while they are at work. An insurance underwriter we recently interviewed explained it this way: "A good work environment is when you wake up on Monday mornings excited for work. A poor one has you staying up Sunday nights worrying about it."

The new leader is the culture builder. Beyond providing direction and purpose, he or she must be the architect of a work environment that stimulates and excites. He needs to ask himself, "What can I do to help them realize their goal of producing high quality? What do I need to do to make this the best job they ever had?"

Primarily, workers must trust that they are free to participate. Fear must be banished and avenues of communication must be wide open. From a purely profit-and-loss point of reasoning, the equation is simple. Without the inspired participation of their employees, companies will continue to be plagued with second-rate internal systems. Without improved systems, product and service defects will continue—a fatal status quo in today's market.

From a customer-relations point of view, the work culture is equally important. The new leader must recognize that employees will treat their customers only as well as they feel they have been treated.

Customers will be served well only as long as employees are encouraged to raise issues and are asked to come up with new ideas and methods of pleasing the customer.

A disgruntled employee working for a traditionally structured insurance company once told us: "If I want to drive my boss crazy, I do exactly what he says."

The new leader understands that he or she cannot mandate customer service. She has to earn it by building a culture that promotes trust, participation, communication, inspiration, and individual empowerment.

As your company or team moves into the 21st century, you will be operating in an environment of greater employee autonomy and self-direction. Teams will be less controlled by upper management and more responsible for completing tasks from start to finish. It will be your job, as a leader, to ensure that your team's efforts are bound together by a shared commitment to a common purpose and set of values.

Paradoxically, as you delegate to the front line, *more* leadership is required of you, not less. A unique reciprocal relationship evolves between leadership and the front line. As the front line takes on greater tactical and operational authority, leaders become ever more responsible for being the source of vision and a healthy work culture.

We once worked with a bank president who enthusiastically embraced this idea. He saw his role as ensuring that everyone in his bank shared his vision of the organization and the culture in which people did their work. He eliminated all first-line supervision in the bank branches and in his administrative departments, replacing it with self-managed teams.

In the midst of the confusion created by these changes, he was surprised at how much more leadership was demanded of him. The move to self-management had eliminated a structure of control that had existed for years. His employees, although given new decision-making responsibilities, were uncertain of their limits. It was his job to define these broad limits as well as to unite his staff behind a common vision.

SECTION

II

BUILDING
THE VISION

The remainder of this book outlines our field-tested action plan. This section contains a step-by-step method to create and powerfully communicate your vision. It describes how to develop the two elements of your vision: the Mission Statement and the Guiding Principles.

Simply writing a Mission Statement isn't enough, however. We will also show you how to share it with the people in your organization so it becomes a vital part of your everyday operation. We will additionally provide you with specific strategies that will enable you to be a walking, talking demonstration of your vision.

3

DRAFTING A VISION STATEMENT: YOUR MISSION STATEMENT

We've observed scores of companies all over the country. In analyzing the relationships between the employees and management and between the employees themselves, we found distinct differences from one company to the next. At first, some of these differences were hard to define. We wrestled with our reaction to one company in particular because it was something we *felt* rather than observed. Finally, we discovered it was in the emotional reactions we had to spending time consulting and training the teams. There were some days when we left a work site breathing a sigh of relief—secretly grateful that we didn't have to work there day after day. For reasons we couldn't quite put our finger on at first, we knew that working there would be damaging to our souls and peace of mind. There was a vague sense of despair and resignation about these places that we sensed, rather than saw.

Other companies had an entirely different feel. The environment was alive and productive. The employees were enthusiastic about their work and about each other. Spending a week with these teams left us energized and excited.

The contrast was remarkable. It wasn't a function of the physical surroundings. Two of the more depressing companies we encountered were housed in beautiful, well-designed offices. So what did account for the differences in these companies? What makes one workplace stimulating, while another is crushing to the human spirit?

It is undoubtedly the most important question future business leaders can ask.

THE CRITICAL VARIABLES

In analyzing vital, energetic companies, we found that their success was almost always driven by the creativity, enthusiasm, and expertise of their entire work force. Digging further, we found that three elements were present in each of these companies. They were:

1. **Shared purpose.** People worked together, their sights elevated above the details of the work itself. They shared a mutual commitment to the goal—the mission—of the company and each individual could articulate that mission.

2. **Shared values.** This is perhaps the most difficult element to define, but it is also one of the most important. We found that even beyond a shared sense of purpose, the people shared values, which guided not only the way each individual treated his or her work, but how they treated one another. These companies had established an internal culture based on trust and participation. This culture fostered creativity and

productivity and enhanced both the employees' work and their lives.

3. **The presence of leadership.** This culture can't be sustained without leadership, however. The employees who worked in the most vital, productive companies all professed a sense of personal connection with the company leaders. It was a connection that inspired commitment to the vision of the company, rather than mere compliance. Leaders, we found, are the keystone to the quality of the work environment. Without enlightened leadership, vision collapses and dies.

DRAFTING YOUR VISION STATEMENT

An undefined vision is much like a bolt of lightning. It may be illuminating for a short time, but it strikes at random and can be dangerous. We haven't figured out a way to bottle lightning yet, but we can capture the energy of a powerful vision.

The bottle we use is called the Vision Statement. It is your single most important tool for leading your company into the 21st century.

The Vision Statement is a carefully prepared document (although "document" does not describe how *alive* a Vision Statement should be) that captures your company's purpose and values. It is the first critical step in making *vision* a reality for every member of the company.

Your Vision Statement should have three components:

1. **The Mission Statement** is a written statement of purpose, crafted to inspire employees to commit to the company's vision.

2. **The Glossary** defines key words and phrases in the Mission Statement; this prevents differing interpretations of the mission.

3. **The Guiding Principles** are the crucial values that guide employees' relationships with customers and one another.

THE MISSION STATEMENT

Writing the Mission Statement will be one of the most important exercises you can ever do with your team or company. Each member of the team will be involved in discussions defining why the company exists in the first place. You will be working together to write a Mission Statement that answers four questions which capture the company's reason for being:

- Who are we?
- What do we do?
- For whom do we do it?
- Why do we do it?

Your Mission Statement has several functions. First, it establishes the purpose of the company. For example, a rapidly growing software company's mission is: "Create and market world-class software that lets people solve problems the way they think about them." After reading that statement of mission, could any employee doubt what his or her goal was in that company?

The second purpose of a Mission Statement is to coordinate actions and efforts. Developed and communicated correctly, it can be a powerful organizing tool, providing essential direction. Those who understand and *believe in* the mission of the company are more likely to work in harmony—like a well-directed orchestra. (It will be a leader's job to make sure that *everybody* understands and commits to the Mission Statement.) Without a powerful Mission

Statement, people in a company will often find themselves working at cross-purposes—a lethal mistake in a competitive market.

But simply stating the goal of the company in a sentence (or paragraph) isn't enough. The Mission Statement itself must be exciting and supercharged with energy. It must inspire and invite commitment. It must be written in such a way that when employees read it they say, "Yes! That is a good reason for me to want to get up and go to work in the morning." It must entice them to make the company's goal their own.

By setting a goal, a Mission Statement also creates a future for the company. This becomes increasingly important as the organization begins to change to meet the demands of the 21st century. As the company begins to unleash authority toward the front lines and the traditional spans of control begin to disappear, the resulting confusion can render the company virtually immobile. A strong Mission Statement is the most important tool you have to ensure this doesn't happen.

For example, we recently worked with a rapidly growing international transportation company. It soon became clear that those in the organization did not know what the vision or the strategic direction of the company was. People described how they agonized for four months over project decisions that should have been routine. They didn't know whether their decisions would move the company forward or not. The ambiguity created by this lack of direction caused huge inefficiencies.

The first thing we had the senior managers of the company do was create a Mission Statement. They determined that their mission was to be the national, low-cost provider of their particular service. By clarifying the company mission as both "national" and "low-cost," company leaders enabled departments to better determine what their role was in moving the company forward.

SHARED MISSION: A FOUNDATION FOR TEAMWORK

A Mission Statement is imperative in companies whose goals are changing. A few years ago, we were asked to mediate a problem in a utility company where two top executives were said to have a personality conflict. One of the men was in his mid-fifties and his entire life had been devoted to the company. He had come to the company in his twenties, starting as a laborer on a line crew. Over the next 30 years he worked his way up to director of sales. He was a gruff man, short, squat, with a rumpled suit and a smelly cigar.

The other man was the director of special projects, though still in his late twenties. He was eager, energized, and dressed for success. On the surface, it appeared as though these two men were born to irritate each other.

The issue they were battling over was simple. The young manager wanted to use the sales force to entice customers to purchase low-cost energy-saving devices, such as insulation blankets for water heaters. He believed that was the best way to serve the company's customers. The older man scoffed at the notion. His vision was that the company had one mission: to sell power.

We pointed out that the problem wasn't between these two men, it was a failure of leadership. Lacking a clear statement of mission by the directors of the utility, each man had arrived at a different understanding. Little wonder they had a "personality conflict."

Like many organizations, the utility company had *no* written Mission Statement. That might have been acceptable in the past, but in today's kinetic market, its absence created the ambiguity of purpose that left two very committed and well-intentioned managers at each other's throat.

The solution? The company put time and effort into developing a Mission Statement, which clearly defined its goals and reason for existing: "... To find and serve as many customers as possible and to help those customers use power responsibly."

Safety Net and Creative Catalyst

In order to reap the astonishing productivity gains that inspired employees can generate, the successful organizations of the future will be designed to stimulate creativity. The Mission Statement does that in two ways.

First, a Mission Statement provides broad boundaries within which people can channel their creativity. We can draw an analogy to children on a playground. It has been observed that when there are no fences around the playground, children tend to group together in the middle of the yard. As soon as a fence is placed around it, they spread out and explore every corner. Much like that fence, a Mission Statement helps define the company's goals and establishes the boundaries for reaching those goals. Given those parameters, people are far freer to exercise and direct their creativity.

The second way the Mission Statement stimulates creativity is through inspiration. It must be catalytic, focusing and igniting action from those who read it. A convincing Mission Statement will touch the hearts of those who read it, and encourage them to take on the company's mission as their own. Because of their personal commitment, they are moved to creatively spend more time, effort, and intensity.

The Seattle-based Nordstrom department store has become a national model for customer service because Nordstrom employees believe in the company's mission. Their Mission Statement, in part, says: "Dedication to customer service is our company's greatest strength."

The type of quality service customers receive at Nordstrom can't be written into a job description. Each employee is continually looking for an innovative way to serve the customers. An associate of ours purchased a suit there on the day before he was to speak at a conference. The suit had to be altered, but the saleswoman told him not to worry. She drove to the conference early the following morning with the suit. She also brought along several ties she thought would be appropriate. She wasn't told to do this by anyone. The creative effort came from her sense of security that she not only could, but was encouraged to, find innovative ways to serve her customers.

Creativity is especially important to any company that deals with a variety of clients. Since every customer is unique, you can't achieve full customer satisfaction by standardizing your company's response to them. You must rely on the creativity of your employees to deal with each different situation differently. By empowering their employees and encouraging them to be inventive within the goals of the company, Nordstrom has achieved one of the highest customer satisfaction ratings in the country.

Speed and Clarity

"There will be two kinds of companies in the future—the quick and the dead," wrote Tom Peters. In the future, the "need for speed" will be paramount to survival. As we discussed in the first two chapters, organizations must be flexible enough to act immediately on new information and provide fast customer service. That means employees at all levels, not just top management, must be able to react and provide quality service. In order to do that, employees will have a wider range of operations and their roles will be less rigidly defined. This change will unleash a remarkable amount of energy that will need to be directed. Again, the Mission Statement may be your best tool to activate and channel that energy.

The final reason that companies of the future need a powerful Mission Statement is that there is likely to be much more ambiguity in employee roles and procedures. This type of uncertainty often leads to conflict and a breakdown in trust. The solution to this potential problem is for leaders to make clear the strategy, direction, and mission of the company.

A national delivery organization we worked with not long ago had taken steps to decentralize decision making and empower the front line. But the company had fallen into a state of confusion. The front line did not know the basic direction and vision of the company.

When the changeover occurred, even though they were told they had more authority, the frontline employees became very suspicious. They weren't sure what upper management was doing or why it was doing it. Most of them suspected that management had a hidden agenda and expressed anger and distrust. What was missing was a clear message from management about the mission of the company. The company leaders needed to find a way to assure the employees that no matter what happened, everyone in the company was on the same side of the net. Management had to convince the front line that they were all operating from the same agenda toward the same goals.

The company recognized the problem and spent several weeks developing a powerful Mission Statement that ultimately convinced the employees that everyone was playing by the same rules and for the same team.

THE ANATOMY OF A MISSION STATEMENT

There is no one correct form for a Mission Statement. In some companies they are a half-page to a page long, while in others they may be only one sentence. (We've listed an excellent example of a company Mission Statement at the end of the chapter.) Generally, the shorter the better, as long as it does the job.

One of the shorter Mission Statements came from a service-oriented company we worked with, whose president had been a fighter pilot in World War II. Once, he was asked to fly an exceptionally hazardous mission where his safety depended on the expert timing of a fellow pilot. When he looked over, the other pilot just said, "I'll be there." (He was and the mission was successful.) Later, that became his company's Mission Statement. It provided a clear message to his employees about the goal of the company and what was expected of them. They were to "be there," both for the company's customers and for each other.

Regardless of its length, a Mission Statement must be:

- memorable
- compelling
- focused on customer service

Some company managers have insisted that the Mission Statement not only be memorable, but memorized as well. When Victor Kiam took over Remington, he knew the company had to change its direction. He realized he had to instill a sense of mission among the employees to increase production. Shortly after buying the company, he developed a Mission Statement. Then he went out on the shop floor and stopped the first employee he saw. He reached into his left pocket and pulled out a $10 bill.

"If you can recite the company's Mission Statement to me, the company will give you the $10," he said. "If not, it goes into the other pocket, which is my pocket." The first week, the employee couldn't do it. Neither could a different employee the next week. The following week and every week thereafter, however, the first employee he asked earned the $10. A year later he figured it was a good investment. "It only costs me $520 a year to make sure everyone in my company knows the company's Mission Statement."

If you ask three or four of your frontline employees (at random) to recite the mission of your company and you do not receive a consistent answer, then in fact you have no mission.

A Mission Statement must also be compelling. It must move people. It must inspire them to personally commit to it. A hospital we worked with developed a Mission Statement that said: "We will care for the physical, spiritual, and emotional needs of our patients." It was enthusiastically embraced by the people who worked there. It meant something to them. It helped clarify that they were committed 100 percent to their patients. The Mission Statement was even shared by the community and became a topic of conversation that led to other discussions—such as how to allocate resources to ensure that all these needs were met. It was an active statement that became a part of the lives of everybody who worked in that hospital.

A Mission Statement must focus on the needs of the customer. It recognizes that it is the customer's needs—and not those of the company's board of directors or executives or managers—that are the most important. This focus on the customer, above and beyond the company's top brass *and even beyond profits,* is one of the biggest changes from the top-down hierarchy. Clear customer focus will not be easy to achieve, but it is necessary if employees are going to be inspired to act creatively and take risks. The purpose and mission of the company must be to serve the customer.

LEADERSHIP ACTION PLAN
DRAFTING YOUR TEAM'S MISSION STATEMENT

PURPOSE OF THIS ACTION PLAN

To create your team's Mission Statement and Glossary.

OVERVIEW OF THIS WORK SESSION

During this session, your team will:

- discuss the importance and use of a Mission Statement.
- create the team's Mission Statement through a variety of group exercises.
- create a Glossary that defines the most important terms and phrases of the Mission Statement.

WHO SHOULD DRAFT THE MISSION STATEMENT?

Even though the end result will be to emphasize frontline participation, drafting your Mission Statement begins as a top-down process. If you are a CEO or senior manager, you may want to consider a group made up of your direct reports. If you run a small business or department, you may want to ask the entire team to attend the meeting.

PLANNING THE WORK SESSION

Read Carefully and Adapt Freely

The action plans presented in this book include techniques we have developed in work with individuals and teams in a variety of companies and disciplines. We have done our best to offer strategies that will work for you. You may decide to implement many of them exactly as written.

We encourage you, however, to feel free to adjust the guidelines to suit your particular situation. In preparing to lead a group session, for example, you may wish to add other discussion topics. You may think of ways to phrase some of our suggested topics that are more suited to your team's culture and normal manner of communication.

We encourage you to experiment. Be sure to plan carefully and always know what you are going to do next if something doesn't seem to work as smoothly as you had hoped.

If Possible, Use a Facilitator to Lead Group Sessions

The action plans describe work to be done by groups. Some of these sessions involve your team. Others involve teams led by managers further down in your reporting structure.

A question arises: When a work session involves a team, who should lead it? The most immediately apparent answer is the team's leader or manager. This *can* work, but we think that a work session led by the team's manager imposes possible limitations on both the leader and the group.

If you lead your team's sessions, you will have to be thinking about what is happening with the group and what needs to happen next. This will limit your ability to take part in the discussion freely as a team member. You may be too busy leading the session to be able to think and listen as undistractedly as you might like.

There will also be times when the quality of the team's discussions will be affected if the team's immediate supervisor is leading the discussion. Some teams find it much easier to speak up if the discussion leader is someone other than their immediate supervisor.

For these reasons, we strongly recommend that you ask someone from outside the group to serve as facilitator. This may be someone from your human resources department or a skilled trainer. This person's job is to keep the meeting focused and moving. By giving this job to someone else, you will be able to participate and not be distracted by the mechanics of running the meeting.

If it is not practical for you to have a facilitator lead this meeting, you *can* lead as well as participate in the discussions successfully. The key to executing both roles is preparation. Study the action plan carefully. Create notes to help you structure the time and to remind you of any comments you want to be sure to make. Know exactly what you intend to do before you do it.

Since you are the boss, the team may allow you to dominate the discussion or look to you to make difficult decisions. Allow plenty of opportunities for others to speak. Make sure you are sharing the airtime and that the team gets the majority of it. Call on others to speak. Ask for opinions. Ask someone to debrief each session with you. Ask the team to be prepared to give you feedback on how you did as a facilitator and to help you generate strategies for improvements in subsequent sessions.

Take Care of Essentials

Successful group work sessions depend on the obvious details being taken care of—every time, without fail. Here is a checklist of things to take care of in planning group sessions:

Attendance. Make sure every team member is available for the session and understands that his or her participation is essential.

Check pagers and cellular phones at the door. No interruptions are to be allowed. Nothing will disrupt the flow of the work quicker than people coming and going for phone calls. This especially applies to *you*.

Have ample supplies on hand. You will need two easels, flip charts, and plenty of fresh pens. Have tape on hand for sticking pages up on the walls.

Place. You want the physical space to be conducive to a relaxed, open, and creative work session. Make sure it is comfortable and well lit. If the only space you have available on-site is a cold and gloomy room, consider renting a meeting room for these group work sessions. This will make it clear that you consider these meetings important.

A Word About Time—and Pace

Writing a Mission Statement is a job that cannot and should not be rushed. You should put aside at least a day for this activity.

You also need patience. You are about to enter into a conversation where there is likely to be disagreement. At times the discussion may be heated; at other times it may drag. Often it may seem that nothing much is being accomplished. This is normal in writing a Mission Statement.

Sometimes you may need to put everything down and walk away from it for a while. This is the incubation or "soak" time. Let it all soak in. It may take more than one day to write an acceptable Mission Statement.

Personal Preparation Before the Meeting

Prior to the initial meeting, set aside time to think about your own feelings about the team's Mission Statement. Clearly, the meeting is designed for the *group* to produce the Mission Statement, but as the leader of the group you want to be prepared to share your own thoughts on the matter.

During this preparation time, you should dig deep and articulate to yourself why you are in this business, what inspires you, and what you hope to accomplish.

Ultimately you need to be able to answer these four questions for yourself: Who are we? What do we do? For whom do we do it? Why do we do it?

During this time you are not committing anything to paper. Rather, you are preparing yourself to speak from the heart. The team members will take their lead from you. If you aren't totally committed, honest, and sincere, they won't be either. Conversely, when you do speak from the heart, it will break down barriers and create the trust needed to make this meeting work.

STRUCTURING THE WORK SESSIONS: THE MISSION STATEMENT AND GLOSSARY

Here are suggested guidelines for structuring the work sessions to create the Mission Statement and Glossary:

Step 1: Describe the Purpose of the Sessions

Begin by explaining the purpose, goals, and procedures for creating the Vision Statement. Note specifically that the Vision Statement consists of a Mission Statement, a Glossary of terms, and Guiding Principles. Distribute copies of the sample Vision Statement that appears at the end of this chapter. Describe this as a project that will take several sessions spread out over an appropriate period of time.

Step 2: Establish the Purpose of This Session

Emphasize the purpose of the first meeting: to begin the development of the unit's Mission Statement and the Glossary defining key terms in the Mission Statement.

Step 3: Request Full Participation

Emphasize that this is not just an exercise, but one of the most important tasks your team will ever perform. This is the time when you must show your personal involvement and commitment to the entire process.

Make it clear that the Vision Statement needs to be a product of the *team's* thinking, not yours. Stress that you want their participation in the creation of a compelling and enduring statement of the team's mission and guiding principles. Ask that this be a no-holds-barred discussion. Differing levels of authority may be represented in the room, but it is imperative that everyone participate. Job titles don't count inside this room—only the thoughts and feelings that are expressed.

If you choose to lead this session for your own team, it is critical that you do not inhibit the full expression of the team. Although most leaders are careful not to overtly dominate meetings, we have witnessed instances where it happened in a totally nonverbal manner. What we sometimes see are managers who sit silently without moving while the discussion begins. As soon as they hear what they want, their eyes light up and they begin to nod their head. Body language alone can have a tremendous effect on the discussion. If you control the group, either through nonverbals or through overt domination of time and discussions, the effort to create a Vision Statement that is crafted carefully and supported by the group will probably fail.

Step 4: Discuss the Importance of Having a Mission Statement

Before you start the work on the Mission Statement, the team must understand why it is important. Lead a discussion of the uses and importance of Mission Statements. Some questions to stimulate discussion are:

- Why is it important to have a Mission Statement?
- Have any of you worked in organizations where a Mission Statement was used effectively?
- How was it used?
- What was its impact?

Use flip charts to focus and summarize group discussions. After you've asked the team why a Mission Statement is important, write down their answers. Often the lists grow to be several pages long.

Some members of the group may express skepticism about whether a Mission Statement is useful. Expect it and don't criticize those members. Everybody must feel comfortable to express whatever he or she feels. Some of them may have already worked in organizations where statements of mission were written on retreats, then filed away and never used. It's likely that most of the members will have some doubts. This is a perfect time to address those doubts and instill the belief that what they are doing is important.

Step 5: Brainstorming Elements of the Mission Statement

Begin listing possible words and phrases to be included in the Mission Statement. Set up two easels with flip charts. Create headings for four open areas on the flip-chart pad (two on each pad) for the four questions posed to the team:

Who are we?

What do we do?

For whom?

Why?

The team should brainstorm these four questions simultaneously, with the facilitator writing down each thought under the appropriate question. Some of the ideas will show up under more than one heading. That's OK. The point of the discussion is to stimulate as many reactions to these questions as possible. The brainstorming should continue until all the thoughts are exhausted.

When the team is finished and all the thoughts have been recorded, ask the team to consider one list at a time. Ask them to evaluate the answers to each question. Underline those that stand out to the group as particularly important. The best answers should be included in the Mission Statement. Those not used in the Mission Statement can possibly be used in creating the Glossary and Guiding Principles.

Step 6: Write Mission Statement Drafts in Small Groups

Break the team up into groups of two or three people. Ask each small group to draft a Mission Statement, based on work done so far by the large group. They can use the sample Mission Statement as one model to consider in their writing but should not feel limited by it.

Give the small groups time to work. This can take up to half an hour. Check on their progress as they work. When most of the groups are nearing completion, give all the groups 10 more minutes to work.

Reconvene the large group and record the various Mission Statements on the flip charts for everyone to see. Ask for the group's reactions to each draft of the Mission

Statement. This should build the team's momentum as they near the most difficult and exciting step.

Step 7: Move Toward Consensus

Encourage all the team members to express themselves in this discussion. Focus attention on the drafts of the Mission Statement and on choosing the best parts of each to complete the final version.

The team needs to reach a true consensus on the final Mission Statement. The wording must be acceptable to every member of the group. This step will take time. Don't try to rush it. It may take two or even three meetings. Encourage the team to stay with it. The reward is just around the corner.

Begin the discussion by asking which parts of the drafts of the Mission Statements they especially like. Often one of the drafts will act as the foundation for the final statement. This discussion should be lively, in-depth, and meaningful. The facilitator can help out by separating the phrases that have been unanimously approved by the team so they can move on to the other parts of the Mission Statement.

Once the drafts have been thoroughly discussed by the team, reconvene the small groups. This time the groups should take the phrases that were approved by the team and compile another draft. These should be placed on the flip charts and again discussed by the entire group.

A final Mission Statement should then be hammered out by the entire group.

The mood of the team should be monitored during this process. If exhaustion sets in or a deadlock occurs, call a halt to the meeting. Let the discussion soak for a while—perhaps a day or two. Then call another meeting and begin again. *Remember: Mission Statements can't be produced by brute force.*

One of the dangers of reaching a consensus is that the Mission Statement can be reduced to the lowest common denominator and thus lose its magic and sparkle. If this happens, start over. While there must be a consensus, the Mission Statement itself must remain compelling. If necessary, appoint a small group to write it so that it excites and motivates.

Step 8: Confirm Commitment to the Mission Statement

The final step is confirming the commitment. This should be done in a ceremonial atmosphere that celebrates both the completion of the Mission Statement and the individual's commitment to it. Confirming the Mission Statement is more than just agreeing to the words, or the way it is structured. It means making a personal, heartfelt commitment to the importance and validity of the Mission Statement.

This can be accomplished in different ways. One of the most effective ways is for each member of the team to stand and comment on the Mission Statement, culminating with his or her approval. The ceremony should be enjoyable and sincere.

Step 9: Create the Glossary

The next task is to write the Glossary, which defines the key words and phrases used in the Mission Statement. The Glossary can be written by a small group within the Mission Statement team.

Begin by posting the Mission Statement on a flip chart and asking the group to identify key words or short phrases that need to be defined. Underline them as this discussion proceeds. The group can then start

brainstorming short definitions, recording them on the
flip chart as they are generated.

See the sample Glossary at the end of this chapter,
which should give you an idea of what your Glossary
should look like.

Step 10: Confirm the Glossary

If the Glossary has been written by a subgroup, ask them to
present their work to the entire team for their discussion
and approval.

Step 11: Create a Finished Product

Once the Mission Statement and Glossary are completed,
they should be dressed up, preferably by someone skilled
in word processing. Create a final draft of the Mission
Statement and Glossary that is visually appealing. This will
be the document you will present to the rest of the people in the company.

Sample Vision Statement

Mission Statement, Glossary, and Guiding Principles

The following Mission Statement, Glossary, and Guiding Principles are based on ones developed by a regional newspaper. They are offered as examples for your team's consideration in writing its own.

Mission Statement

We are the dominant providers of information essential to (our) County, every day meeting the needs of the people we serve.

Glossary of Terms Used in the Mission Statement

We	Each and every one of us. Working together without regard to department boundaries. We are united in our mission. We all influence the result.
Dominant	We always do it better. We have a dominant market share in advertising, readership, and news, which results in revenue growth and reader retention. We are recognized for our outstanding customer service.
Providers	We provide information using all means at our disposal. We incorporate new ideas and adopt new technologies whenever they improve the quality of what we do and expand our information reach.

We provide quality:

- In the information we present.
- In the way we treat our customers.
- In the appearance of our products.

Information We recognize that we are an information company. Information—news and advertising—is our common currency. The information we provide meets the highest standards of quality, honesty, integrity, accuracy, and reliability.

We are a complete newspaper. The information we provide is relevant to the wide variety of communities in the county. We address all of our readers' needs, from global news to information that is useful to them in their daily lives.

Essential We make ourselves essential by keeping pace with change and helping people understand and cope with it. We provide the means for good citizenship and informed decision making. We play an essential role in setting the public agenda by the choices we make and the emphasis we give in selecting and presenting news and opinion. We provide a conduit essential to businesses and consumers, putting us at the center of (our) County's economic life, making us the marketplace where buyers and sellers come together.

County Our focus is the people of (our) County as individuals and in a multitude of roles:

- As voters, citizens, and elected officials.
- As members of occupational, social, and religious groups.
- As readers and advertisers.

- As members of our "forgotten classes," including the homeless, the poor, the elderly, the victims of crime.
- As leaders and residents of the communities in which we live.
- As people anywhere whose lives we touch.

Every day	Tomorrow isn't soon enough. We meet the ever-changing needs of our customers 100 percent of the time. We constantly examine what we do, who we are, and how we do it—every day.
Meeting the needs	We anticipate the needs of the people we serve and are recognized for being customer driven. We cause things to happen in the communities we serve. Our advertisers get results. We retain our readers through service and product. We gain circulation in our targeted areas.
People we serve	Each other, our readers, our subscribers, our advertisers, and the communities within (our) County.

OUR GUIDING PRINCIPLES

Principles that guide our work

- We continually improve the quality of everything we do.
- We are customer driven. Everything we do provides a service. We outperform our competitors in meeting our customers' needs.

- We are accurate and timely.
- We are relevant to people's lives and their community. We bring a sense of order and identity.
- We meet our deadlines.
- We have a sense of urgency in all we do.

Principles that guide our culture

- We rely on the participation and initiative of every single person.
- We have decision making as close to the customer as possible.
- We recognize each other's successes.
- We support the growth of people both personally and professionally.
- We respect the value and contribution of each individual. Every job is essential to our success.
- We communicate openly and honestly.
- We listen.
- We work in partnership with each other.
- We act with integrity, honesty, a sense of ethics. We keep our commitments.

4

Drafting a Vision Statement: Your Guiding Principles

After writing the Mission Statement and Glossary, one final step remains in defining your vision. You will need to develop the specific principles that will guide the work and relationships within your company. Ultimately, these Guiding Principles will emerge as a written list of values. They should be designed to help shape every employee's relationship with the customer and each other.

The most successful companies worldwide are values-driven. That means a bedrock of common, positive values underlies the thinking and the creativity of everyone in those organizations.

The reason we use the term *Guiding Principles* is that the word *values* can lead to confusion. People sometimes react in a negative way to it. They feel that in dealing with "values," the organization is going beyond the work-place into their private lives. It can leave people feeling defensive, when the motive behind the process is to do just the opposite. *Guiding Principles* is a much friendlier term.

Developed correctly, the Guiding Principles will encourage trust on all levels. The Mission Statement sets a goal for the company; the Guiding Principles explain *how* to achieve that goal in two areas.

First, they establish the professional standards for the work done inside the organization. Without clear standards, the organization may suffer inconsistent efforts, because people don't know what level to strive toward. The Guiding Principles establish a clear level of quality and excellence that every employee can understand and aspire to maintain.

The other area in need of Guiding Principles is the relationships between the people in the organization—on all levels. We define this intricate and complex set of human interactions as the organization's *culture*. Every organization has a culture. If ignored, it will emerge by itself, undirected and often counterproductive. On the other hand, if consciously created and nurtured, it will add vital strength and creativity to the organization. Building and sustaining an empowering organizational culture is your biggest and most important challenge as a new leader. Organizations without a thriving, fear-free, and productive culture will fail.

The Mission Statement sets goals; the Guiding Principles shape the culture necessary to achieve those goals.

The Guiding Principles are especially important as top-down hierarchies give way to self-managed teams. As you unleash authority to the front line, the Guiding Principles are often all people have left (and all they need, if done correctly) to show them *how* to accomplish the organization's mission.

Without an articulated set of Guiding Principles, your vision will struggle on its journey toward becoming a shared mission throughout the organization. A set of agreed-upon values can galvanize an organization. It is the game plan that coordinates everyone's efforts toward the same goal. It strengthens and nurtures. It provides security and allows and encourages every employee to express passion toward his or her work and commitment to the organization's mission.

The Mission Statement plus the Guiding Principles form the foundation of your organization's culture. They include the values that guide the work as well the values that guide employees' relationships with each other. The values of all world-class companies have six cultural elements in common:

1. *Passionate customer focus.* Companies succeed or fail according to how committed they are to fulfilling the customer's needs. In successful companies, the customer is foremost in the mind of every person in the company, and therefore traditional organizational charts are being turned upside down. Rather than senior management on top, the customer is boss. Next in priority are the frontline employees. The leadership of the company forms the foundation on which this inverted pyramid rests.

   Whether a company has abandoned its hierarchical mind-set in favor of a focus on the customer will be the acid test for success in the future.

   We can tell very quickly whether an organization has succeeded in making this transition. We simply approach a frontline employee and ask him or her: "Who do you need to please in order to succeed here?"

   What we usually hear is: "I need to please my boss."

   That is the wrong answer.

   That hierarchical mind-set distracts companies from the customers' needs. In the successful companies we've worked with, the answer is always:

"Who do I need to please? My customer, of course."

2. *Urgent obsession with quality.* Winning organizations have in common these four simple ideals:

- Satisfy the customers 100 percent of the time.
- Make zero mistakes.
- Generate no waste.
- Do this every day.

This is a far cry from the reality in most American businesses, where 25 to 40 percent of the average operating budget is spent on finding and correcting mistakes.

As we have pointed out, however, many companies around the world are approaching these goals. Any company that hopes to succeed in the 21st century must do the same.

3. *Continuous improvement.* The old adage "Success is a journey, not a destination" applies here. Winning companies are not static. They are always changing, growing, improving. This is especially true when it comes to continuous improvement of the internal culture. Continuous improvement doesn't mean massive change in this case, but rather an unending series of small enhancements. This idea needs to be constantly reinforced, because it is in opposition to the traditional American inclination to want to hit the grand slam.

In the past, the idea of improving a company most often included a "quality drive" meant to turn the organization upside down in six months. We looked for a dramatic breakthrough, an innovation that would magically propel the organization into the 21st century.

It doesn't work that way.

Winning companies are often thin on the dramatics. What they have instead is a relentless desire to improve—day by day, week by week, year by year. Leadership must underscore the concept of continuous improvement until it becomes part of the fabric of the organization. The only enduring competitive edge is to learn to do things better faster than your competition.

There is a company that manufactures automobiles in the United States and in Japan. Not long after the company began doing business in this country, the company's leadership became concerned because it noticed that the transmissions of the U.S.-made cars broke down, while those made in Japan did not. The company dispatched a team to determine the reasons. In studying the U.S. plant the team found that all of the parts were within the quality specifications established—plus or minus 0.05 of an inch of the target. The problem was that although every part was within the specs, the sum of the total deviations added up to a defective transmission. The American plant was hitting the target and still producing a poor product because the quality process stopped at 0.05.

When the team first studied the Japanese plant, they thought their calibration equipment was broken. Every part they measured was on target. A closer look revealed that the parts did vary—up to 0.002 of an inch. To the workers in the Japanese plant, however, even a 0.002 variance was unacceptable. The teams that were making these parts had been meeting every day to discuss how to reduce the variation. Their next goal was to drop it to 0.001 of an inch. Clearly, these daily meetings were not meant to achieve overnight results. They did, however, lead to fantastic improvements in quality over the long run.

4. *High levels of participation.* Empowering employees by driving decision-making responsibilities to the front lines must be a dynamic and often-discussed value within the organization. Overcoming the mind-set created by nearly a century of top-down authority is not easy, however. Even those who benefit from the change will at times resist because it departs so radically from what they know. Those who feel they are losing power, primarily frontline supervisors, will resist even more. It will be up to the new leaders to promote and exemplify this value on a daily basis.

One of the benefits of unleashing authority is increased employee participation in the organization. More than ever before, organizations need to mine the wisdom of their workers, especially those closest to the action. Improved business and production methods are the direct result of full worker participation. The Japanese have muscled their way to the top of several worldwide industries because their manufacturing methods are more efficient. They are more efficient because they are continually improved by frontline workers who daily are encouraged to make quality recommendations.

Remember, a Japanese autoworker is more than 4,000 times more likely to have a suggestion implemented than an American worker! Successful American companies such as Levi Strauss and others have already awakened to that fact. They understand that to reach their full potential, companies must have the commitment and participation of every single employee.

5. *Teamwork.* Much of the authority unleashed to the front lines is being driven to individuals who work in teams. A major problem in traditional companies has been a lack of communication between individuals and teams. The importance of teamwork and effective team relationships must therefore be continually stressed. At the heart of this value is an articulation of

how, as employees and human beings, we should treat one another. The Guiding Principles should answer the questions: What is expected of each of us? How can we best work together and still maintain individual creativity and productivity?

These aren't simple questions to answer. They will probably take some time. It is important that the answers—shaped in the form of the Guiding Principles—be straightforward, yet as complex and sophisticated as the human relationships they value.

6. *Ethics and integrity.* People must believe in their organization. This may seem an obvious value, but it is one that is often abused. Include in your Guiding Principles the statement that ethics and integrity are the cornerstone of your company. An uncorrected breach of ethics—especially by management—can irreversibly destroy employee commitment.

There are a number of other Guiding Principles you may want to include. For example:

- Qualities of leadership—what is expected of you as a leader?

- Listening—the importance of people listening to one another and of management listening to staff.

- Teaching—some organizations may choose to emphasize ongoing training and improvement.

- Feedback—underscoring the need to constantly talk to each other, especially when it comes to honest evaluations of the effectiveness of the teams.

- Conflict resolution—emphasizing the way conflicts between employees, teams, and management are to be resolved. This doesn't have to spell out the actual process, but rather that it will always be done in a spirit of professionalism.

The Guiding Principles and mission you create for your company will be unique. They will define the character of

your organization. During this process, you should feel
free to express the principles that most go to your heart.
Concentrate on the Guiding Principles that are most per-
tinent to your business. In one way or another, however, if
you want to compete on a world-class level, you must include some variation of these essential six we've listed
above.

THE NEED FOR GUIDING PRINCIPLES

You set something positive in motion when you put the
Guiding Principles down on paper. For senior management, the principles become promises that you make. It
is as if you are saying out loud to every employee: "We
promise that we will behave consistently according to these
guidelines and they will become the reality within this
company—with no exceptions."

If you don't keep that promise you will squander your
capital with your employees. But if you live by your Guiding Principles, you will create the most important cultural
value of all: trust. Without trust, you can't accomplish anything. With trust, your successful relationships will lead to
achieving corporate objectives.

If you keep the promises stated in the Guiding Principles, you will create an atmosphere that encourages creativity and commitment. The trust your employees have
in the organization produces the opportunity for them to
take risks—to search for innovative solutions—because
they gather strength from the security they feel.

A trusting atmosphere also allows for change. It increases people's flexibility and willingness to depart from
old ways of doing things. It also increases their ability to
work through the potential confusion caused by the unleashing of authority. Their tolerance of ambiguity will be
higher because even though their job responsibilities may
be shifting, the Guiding Principles are there to help them
stay on course.

Articulating the Guiding Principles can have a powerful personal effect on each employee. By stating what the organization stands for in an inspiring way, you invite commitment on a personal level. Written correctly, the principles will move each person to say: "Yes, I want to be a part of that."

Organizations that have a strong commitment to their values will stay on course during tough times. An environment based on values nourishes the human spirit and brings out the best in every employee. It makes it easier for everyone's larger, more positive self to thrive.

As we mentioned, your efforts to develop the Guiding Principles may initially be met with resistance. Some people will fear that the company has become too personal and even invasive of your own beliefs. Some may have worked in organizations where company leaders came on like Big Brother or preached values that they themselves didn't live by.

You have to make it clear from the outset that you are not trying to tell your employees how to run their lives. The Guiding Principles you are discussing deal only with the business. You must assure them that articulating these values is only part of an effort to establish a work environment that will be beneficial to everyone—one that will encourage individual thought and action.

You should point out, however, that company and individual values *will* intersect. Many of the values within the Guiding Principles are personal because they deal with each person's relationship with the customer and with fellow workers. This intersection should occur on as broad a base as possible so that deeply felt personal convictions are in alignment with the goals of the organization.

COMMON VALUES ALLOW FOR CHANGE

Teams will work better if they have a common foundation of values. This is especially important when your goals are to meet customer needs 100 percent of the time, making no mistakes and creating no waste.

Once these common values are established and accepted, far less top-down observation is required, because organizational standards and individual responsibilities are clear. This understanding allows a greater movement toward self-managed teams. The shared vision—the mission and the values—binds people together in a much more powerful way than the exhortations of management could ever do. In fact, in the flatter organizations of the future, management exhortations will no longer play much of a role. The controls that ensure the success of a business will come from the universal understanding of the basic philosophy and purpose of the organization.

All of us have a vision. Individually, we each have a sense of purpose and a set of values. Weakness results when these beliefs are scattered or left to work against each other. Successful organizations harness the strength of these beliefs as a collective force.

LEADERSHIP ACTION PLAN
DRAFTING YOUR TEAM'S GUIDING PRINCIPLES

PURPOSE OF THIS ACTION PLAN

To create a list of your team's Guiding Principles.

OVERVIEW OF THIS WORK SESSION

During this work session, your team will:

- discuss the importance of articulating values in the form of Guiding Principles.
- create a list of them in small- and large-group discussions.
- reach agreement on their final wording before joining them with the Mission Statement and Glossary to complete the Vision Statement.

WHO SHOULD DRAFT THE GUIDING PRINCIPLES?

This action plan describes the steps to be taken to complete the work on your Vision Statement. Those who participated in writing the Mission Statement and Glossary should attend this work session.

STRUCTURING THE WORK SESSION

Step 1: Explain the Purpose of This Session

Begin by describing the purpose of the session: to complete the Vision Statement by creating a list of the team's

Guiding Principles. The Guiding Principles are those values that serve as the foundation of the work the company does and the culture of the company itself. Refer the team to the sample Vision Statement at the end of Chapter 3.

The same guidelines apply to this meeting that applied to the previous meetings. You expect full participation and encourage no-holds-barred discussions. Reemphasize, if necessary, that discussions should be unaffected by the differing layers of management in the room.

Step 2: Define and Discuss the Terms

Lead a discussion on the importance of Guiding Principles and further define the term. Emphasize that you are talking about creating two distinct sets of values, just as in the sample Vision Statement. One set refers to those values every member of the firm needs to bring to producing the work you do together. The other set refers to those values all employees need to bring into their working relationships with one another, with a mutual commitment to creating a healthy and productive workplace culture. These Guiding Principles will ultimately be put in the form of short declarative sentences.

Once you are satisfied that the team understands the substance and form of the Guiding Principles, encourage a discussion of why they are important. Ask whether others have worked in organizations where Guiding Principles were used or where certain values were emphasized. How were they used? What was the result?

Be prepared for (and don't discourage) arguments against Guiding Principles. There are usually some fears among the team—where they are expressed or not—that the organization may be attempting to force values on them. These fears need to be addressed. This is a point where you can either win them over or lose them. The team must be assured that these will be *their* Guiding Principles, not yours. They are being created to encourage a fear-free, productive, and supporting environment. They are not simply another set of rules.

Step 3: Do Some Brainstorming

Before you enter into the free-flowing process of actually creating the Guiding Principles, each member of the team should have a completed copy of the Mission Statement and the Glossary.

Now you are ready to begin brainstorming. We suggest you use two flip charts. One is for the Guiding Principles regarding the work itself; the other is for the Guiding Principles for the culture.

Begin by focusing on the Guiding Principles regarding the work itself. Be prepared to summarize on the flip chart the group's discussion of these questions:

- What are some of the most important values we want all employees of this company to bring to the work they do?
- What values lie at the heart of some of the most important promises we make to our clients?
- What values serve as the hallmark of our service (or product)?
- What values might best capture our reputation and how we want to be seen by our customers in the marketplace?

Move to the flip chart labeled "Guiding Principles for Our Culture" and record key points made in the discussion of the following questions:

- What characteristics do we need to bring into our relationships with one another in order to reach the highest levels of quality and best serve our customers?

- What characteristics do we need to bring into our relationships with one another in order to create the most satisfying work environment possible?
- What are some of the most important qualities management needs to bring to its leadership responsibilities?
- Do we want to make mention of any special values with respect to teamwork? Conflict management? Participation?

Before completing this step, post a flip chart listing the six essential components of Vision:

Qualities of guiding principles related to the work itself

- Extreme customer focus
- Sense of urgency
- Continuous improvement

Qualities of guiding principles related to the culture

- High levels of participation
- Teamwork
- Ethics and integrity

Give the group the opportunity to make sure all six are adequately represented in their work in these sessions so far. Some may have already been included in the Mission Statement and Glossary. Any that have been left out, or haven't been addressed in the detail the team desires, should be included on either of the flip charts.

Next, move on to any other values the team feels are important. These are entirely optional and need to reflect the culture and work environment this team is dedicated to creating. They could include special promises that everyone must hold to regarding the quality of the work, or special elements they might wish to bring into their relationships with each other.

At this point, you are still brainstorming and the team shouldn't worry about the exact wording of any of these concepts. You are going for quantity. You want all the ideas on the table.

Exhaust this discussion. Then give the team 24 hours of soak time, reconvene the meeting, and brainstorm again. Make sure everyone has contributed.

Step 4: Refine the Terms

With all the values visible, it is time to look at each one. As you begin, you may find the team wrestling with the problem of which verb tense to use when writing down these values. Use present tense. We have found that short, declarative, present-tense statements make the most powerful presentation.

For example, a simple (but important) Guiding Principle is: "We recognize achievement and those who earn it." If that is not currently the case in your company, you will find that your team will try to word it in the future tense. "We *will* recognize achievement and those who earn it."

The future tense is a hedge. People will want to use it to protect themselves from the gap that exists between the ideal of the Guiding Principles and the reality of the company. If that gap exists in your organization, it is doubly important that you word it in the present tense. It becomes a promise to employees that this value is already becoming a reality. Recognizing the gap and implementing ways to close it shows your strength and commitment as a leader.

Encourage people to suggest Guiding Principles for values they would like to see as a reality but which the company is currently falling short of. The articulation of Guiding Principles is a way for the team to consciously create the qualities of work and culture they would ideally like to see.

One successful senior manager we know has a favorite example that underscores how important it is to close the gap. It occurred in 1960, when NASA launched one of the first moon shots. The rocket was off course from the time it was launched, but when it reached the moon it was perfectly on target. The reason was the NASA team of scientists recognized the gap between where it was heading and its target and applied continuous corrections.

When you begin wording these Guiding Principles, which tell the world who you are and how you act, you should be prepared for discussions about any gaps that may exist in your company. The dynamics of that discussion will help identify where the company needs correction. Implementing those corrections will add great strength to the organization and foster trust among the staff.

Continue to refine the suggested Guiding Principles. Each should represent a separate concept. Don't worry about the number. We've found that on average you will produce 6 to 12, and that a number of specific statements are far more effective than a few generally worded ones. Detail is useful.

For example, rather than saying, "Teamwork is valuable," say, "We relate to each other in a trusting, truthful way." While the intention of the Mission Statement is to be short and memorable, the intention of the Guiding Principles is to *teach*.

Don't limit the number during the brainstorming period, however, because not all will make the final cut.

Step 5: Make Choices

Once the brainstorming is over, go to the flip charts and ask the team to identify which values stand out. This will probably trigger a vigorous discussion. You may ask the team to list the values in order of importance or just to list the top six or eight concepts. Some may be combined into one. However you decide to do it, now is the time for the team to make some choices.

Ask the group to choose those values that should make the short list. As they discuss this topic, circle the values that seem to get broad support.

Step 6: Edit in Small Groups

Once the top values have been chosen, break the team into small groups of two or three people. Each small group will be assigned to edit an equal portion of the Guiding Principles, agreeing on a suggested final wording of the principles to be presented to the whole group. They should write their finished products on the flip-chart paper so the entire group can read them later. (If the word-smithing is done at a separate meeting, the groups can bring back typed copies.)

When this step is finished, the team should be reconvened to do the final editing as a group.

Step 7: Move Toward Consensus

As with the Mission Statement, the team needs to arrive at a consensus about the Guiding Principles. All the participants need to feel they have been able to express themselves fully. Ultimately, they must all support the written documents. Most likely, this part of the process will take time.

Once again, as you move toward consensus, be careful not to lose the magic of the wording. The Guiding Principles should be written in an inspiring way that encourages people to stretch to reach an ideal.

If necessary, you may wish to reconvene the small groups to further edit and clarify one or more of the principles.

When a consensus is reached on all the principles, each individual on the team must confirm his or her commitment to them. This can be done in a ceremonial fashion much as it was done in the Mission Statement process.

5

DO YOUR WALKING
BEFORE YOUR TALKING

Congratulations! You have just completed a critical first step, creating a Vision Statement. You now have a Mission Statement, a Glossary, and Guiding Principles.

It's a great start, but you can't stop here. Just writing them down isn't enough.

Not long ago we were talking to the director of the data processing department of a multinational firm about productivity problems in the department. The director was worried about employee morale and what he feared was a universal lack of commitment. His top assistant was also at the meeting. When we asked them whether they had a mission and sense of purpose defined for the department, the assistant said: "Yes, we do. Last year we developed a Mission Statement in a project with a management team."

The director of the department turned to his assistant with a look of surprise. "We did?" he asked. "Where is it?"

The assistant thought for a moment and shrugged. "I know we filed it around here someplace," he said.

Their problem was obvious. First, they had considered the process merely an exercise. They had just gone through the motions of developing a Mission Statement, then filed and forgot it and reverted back to business as usual. It was a clear sign to their employees that they did not mean what they said. The result was the director lost credibility and the entire department suffered a drop in motivation and inspiration.

We've dealt with other companies that have done the same thing and the result has always been the same. Management loses credibility and the employees feel cheated.

Writing the Vision Statement is only the first step. The second step—making sure that your vision "takes" throughout the organization—is equally vital.

A LIVING DEMONSTRATION

Before taking the Vision Statement out to the front lines, company leadership must first become a living demonstration of the mission and Guiding Principles. In a large company, this will probably be the CEO and his or her direct reports. It could also be a management think tank given the responsibility of handling the process. In smaller companies, it may be the entire management team.

Senior managers must prepare themselves to be effective communicators. There are many reasons for this private preparation. First, a number of skills and steps are required to manage the change created by the Vision Statement. Managers must be ready to deal with that change, both within themselves and within the employees.

Second, the senior managers must achieve a common ground of understanding about the meaning of the Vision Statement and how it will be put into practice. It is essential that they come to a consensus on these issues. The Vision Statement is an ideal: what the company *will* be like and how people *will* treat each other. As a matter of course, gaps between this ideal and the current reality will be exposed. As we have mentioned, these gaps can be damaging if they aren't closed quickly. The way to reduce this danger is for senior management to make its actions consistent with the Vision Statement *before* releasing it.

For example, if one of your Guiding Principles is "We listen to each other," you'll want to ensure that every member of your senior management team does, in fact, listen to his or her staff. Otherwise, when you begin discussing this value among the staff, you will be met with hostility, frustration, and, ultimately, cynicism.

It's important to stress to the senior team that the spreading of the vision should be done quietly, with as little hoopla as possible. Hyping it only sets up resistance. Rather, from the beginning let your actions speak louder than your words. Senior managers must spend time together to learn to model, demonstrate, teach the values themselves.

Senior Team Goals

EMOTIONAL COMMITMENT. Some members of the senior team may go along with the Vision Statement just because there is a lot of momentum in that direction. Don't let that happen. Everyone on the team must be fully committed to making the vision a reality. Otherwise, the cascading process to the front line will break down. If managers lack full commitment, there is no way they can expect it from those they lead.

You need to spend time talking to all the members of the senior management team to make sure they fully understand their role in making the vision a reality—and to ensure they are 100 percent committed to it.

Obviously, the most common problem in getting the senior team to accept the changes is their fear of losing their authority and control. This is a big change for them, and on the surface it will appear as if they *are* losing their power and position, which some of them may have spent years achieving. Many, whether they understand it consciously or not, rely on their elevated place in the top-down hierarchy as a measure of success and even self-worth. Don't underestimate how hard it will be for some of them to make this change.

In a real sense, you will be asking them to raise their consciousness (some will already be there, of course). Point out that rather than pinning their self-esteem to the organizational chart, they are becoming real leaders by enabling people to lead themselves.

This part of the process will be one of your most difficult and important challenges. Spend as much time discussing this issue as you need. Be sure that everyone has expressed all the feelings he or she may have about this. Expect a wide range of emotions—from doubt, frustration, and anger to excitement and exhilaration. Don't let anyone off the hook. This is a time when you must address all the issues and build toward a consensus.

ESTABLISHING TRUST.   Once the management team is ready, it's time to begin to lay a foundation of trust among the frontline employees. The most important element in this foundation is credibility. The senior team's actions must be consistent with their words. When the Vision Statement (consisting of the written Mission Statement, Glossary, and Guiding Principles) is released, it proclaims that certain values are paramount in your organization. These values *must* be reflected in the actions of senior management.

For example, you are asking management to unleash authority. Managers must do this through action and demeanor. In other words, they must not only give more authority to their teams, they must listen carefully to what each person has to say. Conflicts must be resolved in mature ways that show respect for all sides. In general, senior managers must consistently exhibit the values of the Guiding Principles. Chief among these are creating a fear-free environment where every employee is encouraged to participate in a spirit of equality and teamwork. Nothing will sabotage the entire effort faster than for a manager to say one thing and do another.

An obvious example of this hypocrisy is the manager who encourages participation, then trashes an employee who supports an opposing idea. Other examples are more subtle. We've witnessed a number of managers who say they value others' speaking up but who rarely listen to anything anyone has to say. They are used to speaking endlessly and taking up all the airtime for themselves.

In short, you need to make it clear that the job descriptions of your senior team have been rewritten. Gone is the old top-down hierarchy with its simplistic notion of the omniscient boss. As new leaders facing worldwide competition, your management team is being challenged with a new set of values and possibilities. Those teams that accept the challenge and fully understand the multitude of rewards (ranging from skyrocketing productivity to personal enrichment) will create a positive and powerful momentum.

LEADERSHIP ACTION PLAN
SENIOR MANAGEMENT PREPARATION

So far in this chapter, we have been concerned with *why* your senior management team needs to prepare privately before taking the Vision Statement company-wide. The rest of the chapter is devoted to *how* the team should prepare itself.

As we have mentioned, you should plan for this series of meetings with your senior staff (both group and one-on-one) to take several weeks. It should be a thorough exploration of the Vision Statement. Each person on the team should ask himself or herself what it means personally and what it means to the company.

There are two primary goals you should accomplish during these meetings. The first is to embed the vision in the thinking of every manager on the team. The second is to charge each manager to use his or her creativity to identify ways to close the gaps we have discussed: the disparities between the culture described in the Vision Statement and the current reality of the company.

As opposed to the process for developing the Mission Statement and Guiding Principles, where we recommend a step-by-step agenda, be flexible during your senior team meetings. You may want to discuss certain topics, then return to them weeks later and discuss them again. You need to continue with the meetings, however, until the senior management team has reached an agreement about and understanding of what the Vision Statement means and how it is to be implemented.

The following are some topics that are likely to generate some compelling discussions. They may help you break the ice in the initial senior team meetings.

1. *Accomplishing the mission.* Each member should have a copy of the Vision Statement (Mission Statement, Glossary, and Guiding Principles). Take a moment and allow everyone to reread it. Ask them for examples of actions they have taken that have been congruent with the Vision Statement. For example, what recent decisions have they made with an eye toward being consistent with the stated vision? Ask everyone to share examples. They may want to talk about a special case of customer service, or higher productivity resulting from improved systems. The discussion itself will lead to a heightened understanding of the Mission Statement.

Next, ask team members to bring up examples of areas where the company is operating inconsistently with the Mission Statement. Ask them to identify the gaps that exist between the stated ideal of the Mission Statement and the reality of the operation. Take time to dissect the examples. Determine what happened, the cause of the problem, and possible solutions. Most important is to ask whether this issue is indicative of any larger issue in the company that needs to be resolved.

This discussion has a number of purposes. It increases the team's awareness of the gaps and provides some guidance on how to close them. Stress that closing these gaps will help build credibility when the team is ready to take the Vision Statement to the front line.

2. *Discuss each Guiding Principle.* Have the team take a close look at what every Guiding Principle means to them on a personal basis. Follow the same pattern as you did for the Mission Statement. Ask what each of them has done to act consistently with that value. What was the specific incident? What did he or she learn as a result?

Next, ask where they may have fallen short of a particular value. Was there a time when they didn't listen to an employee? What do they need to do the next time to work in harmony with the Guiding Principles? Again, identify gaps in the company for each value. What can be done to eliminate the gaps?

You may want to end the discussion by asking the team what they need from you personally. Do they need more time discussing either the Mission Statement or the Guiding Principles? Do they fully understand their role in the new organization? Are there any lingering doubts? Now is the time to dispel them.

Offer examples of how you have been using the Guiding Principles in your own daily actions and decision making. In the spirit of teaching through sharing experiences, describe the actions you took that supported a given value.

One example that stands out for us involves a retail organization we worked with, where a high priority was placed on the way the place looked to the customer. During slow times, one of the managers would enlist any staff members available for what he called an "impeccability tour." They would walk through the store looking for examples of where the store *was* perfect and areas where they might make improvements. As you might expect, the store was indeed impeccable. As a result of customers finding it aesthetically pleasing, the store has enjoyed robust growth and profits.

3. *Ideals of leadership.* This step involves a detailed discussion about the ideal characteristics, philosophies, and behaviors of leaders in the company. As the senior team discusses the Vision Statement, ask them what they are learning about the qualities needed to be a visionary leader in the new organization. What kinds of characteristics will it take to succeed in this company in the future? This discussion should unfold over several meetings. Give it some comfortable leisure time, because it can yield a wealth of understanding.

It is important that your management team really spend time on this, thinking about what it means to them as people and as leaders in the company. The team might want to develop a written summary that captures their thoughts about leadership. It could be a loose compilation of leadership qualities or a simple statement of how this change affects them directly. This discussion leading to the summary should be heartfelt and honest. The discussion itself may be the most important thing to come from this process, and the document will prove useful as a future reference guide.

TOUGH CHOICES

As a team leader, you need to do everything possible to ensure that your team is behaving consistently with the Mission Statement and the Guiding Principles before those documents are distributed to the rest of the organization.

It is possible, however, that you will encounter one or more managers who don't understand (or don't want to understand) the new vision. This resistance is not unusual. A Vision Statement creates a new yardstick against which to measure the success of a manager. You may have managers, even senior managers, who have succeeded by the old yardstick, but who fail against the new one because it is focused more on culture and the interpersonal aspects of leadership. For example, you may have a manager who is unwilling to remove himself or herself from the details of everyday decision making, and thus whose behavior is inconsistent with the new form of leadership that is required. At this point, you have some options.

First, you may wish to schedule some intensive one-on-one meetings with the troubled manager or team member. This can include personal coaching or teaching while he or she is on the job. Let him know exactly what it is about his behavior that concerns you or is inconsistent with the Mission Statement or Guiding Principles. Find out what the values mean to this person and work with him to

develop corrective action plans. Make sure these are implemented. You can handle the coaching yourself, or you
can enlist a consultant to act in your stead.

If these steps fail, your options become more difficult,
but you still have room to be creative. One company we
observed had drafted a Vision Statement that placed a
high value on personal relationships and empowerment of
frontline employees. One senior manager, however, who
had years of experience and possessed a large number of
important technical skills, could not make the changeover.
He was abusive and abrasive and refused to give up his authority. He was the proverbial bull in the china shop. The
company leader met with him personally and even paid
for professional counseling and training sessions, but he
refused to change. The leader was left with a dilemma. If
he fired the man, the organization would lose some valuable experience and expertise.

Because it was a large organization, the leader was able
to find a nonmanagement position in which the recalcitrant employee could still exercise his technical abilities
without the need for close teamwork with any other
worker.

Sometimes termination will be necessary, however. In
some isolated cases, you will have no choice. When you
talk about your vision, your employees will look at what
you *do* even more than what you say. They will be watching to see whom you promote (or demote) and why. If a
manager—even a senior manager—refuses to accept the
new vision, he or she must be dealt with quickly. Otherwise, your credibility will be seriously undermined. Terminating an employee who does not accept the new vision
underscores your commitment to it and to the organization. It makes a strong statement.

Fortunately, this is the exception rather than the rule.
The percentage of people who don't respond to personal
attention and training is usually very small.

By the end of this chapter, you will have completed a
series of meetings with your senior management team.

They should all thoroughly understand and support the Vision Statement. They will already be taking steps to make this vision a reality. At this point, the management team should be excited and ready to embrace the challenge of taking the vision to the rest of the company.

6

CASCADING THE VISION

Now that your senior team is fully prepared, it's time to take the Vision Statement to the rest of the organization. We call the process "cascading" because the image it conjures up—a powerful and expanding waterfall—captures the dynamics of how the vision should flow throughout your company.

The process is not complicated. But it is not always easy. It is simple in the sense that there are not many steps to take. It is difficult because they must be done correctly to make vision a priority that is both important and urgent throughout the company.

It will be during the cascading process that you as a leader will take your first steps in the unfamiliar territory you entered when you redefined what a leader is and does. Don't let it throw you. If you do what is discussed in this chapter, you will be doing the work of leaders. Much of effective leadership—especially during this time of change—means wearing your values on your sleeve; making them public and observable.

Natural Laws

Over the years, we've noticed that when companies attempt to make significant internal changes, certain truisms stand out. We call them our *Natural Laws of Organizations.* You will find it helpful to understand these natural forces and how to harness them for your own use.

Natural Law 1: You Get What You Talk About

The first Natural Law involves the amount of airtime a company gives to any new idea it is trying to emphasize. Airtime refers to organized discussions, written memos, and official reports. It also refers to casual communications, which often have more cultural impact. During the cascading process, this will include the Mission Statement and the values stated in Guiding Principles.

Stop for a moment and think about what currently gets the airtime in your company. In most organizations, it's the numbers: schedules, profits, expenses, deadlines, and so on. Most organizations spend their company time talking about the technical side of the business. In traditional businesses, cultural values are rarely, if ever, discussed and the company's mission is the domain of only the top management.

If the cascading of the Vision Statement is to be effective, it must get airtime! *You get what you talk about.* Airtime makes up much of the Vision Statement implementation plan. Prepare to spend time every week stressing mission and values to the entire company.

An example of giving a value airtime is the term "good neighbor," which even as you read this you have probably associated with the State Farm Insurance Company. The phrase is an effective advertising slogan, in no small part because it is a value, a *promise* the company is making to its customers and to its employees. "Good neighbor" is also a phrase that is used internally in connection with customer service and even as a value looked for in prospective employees. The company lets it be known that it wants employees who will make good neighbors. It is a clear and simple value. Most important, the company sees to it that the phrase gets *ample and continued* airtime.

Within the company it is far from being just a slogan. It is engraved on the hearts and minds of senior management, middle management, and frontline employees. People at all levels of the company talk about it. It serves as a decision-making yardstick. Employees ask themselves, "What would a good neighbor do in this situation?" It has become a rule of thumb that people bring to solving even technical problems. It is a powerful organizing influence. It inspires each person to do his or her best. As a result of finding the right value, stating it in a compelling way, and giving that value airtime, State Farm has managed to thrive in one of the most competitive industries in the nation.

AIRTIME MUST BE A LINE ACTIVITY.   Conversations about vision must be seen as coming from management. It is impossible to overemphasize this point. What is being discussed here is a profound organizational change. Changes of this magnitude cannot be seen as coming from the human resources department or an external consultant. They must be driven by line management or they will be discounted.

The cascading process must come down from the lines of authority within the company. Workers should primarily hear about vision firsthand from their immediate supervisors. Vision should be a part of the weekly conversations supervisors have with their employees about goals, problems, performance, and values. Everything will be evaluated as to whether it contributes to accomplishing the mission and is consistent with the values of the Guiding Principles. These conversations cannot be delegated away. People must have these conversations with their boss.

By now your managers should know that implementing the vision will be an integral part of their job. Companies are not like governments. The American, French, and two Russian revolutions proved that if people are tired of their governments, they can topple them and create new ones. In business, of course, it doesn't work that way. The only way the hierarchical mindset will be diminished is from the top. The internal culture of any organization is a result of top management. Management can choose to ignore the culture and let it grow without direction, or it can help create a participative and productive culture, unleashing authority and empowering its employees. But for better or worse—directed or undirected—*the culture of a work team is a reflection of its leader.*

Natural Law 2: The Culture of a Work Team Is a Reflection of Its Leader

When a manager doesn't listen or plan, there is no listening or planning within that team. Moreover, if a manager isn't moved by the Vision Statement, it will not take within that team. Conversely, a manager who is creative and inspired and encourages full participation will lead a motivated, highly productive team. This is true whether we are talking about the CEO, with the whole company in his or her focus, or the supervisor on the loading dock with a team of five.

LOOKING *UP* THE ORGANIZATION. Many times we have been asked to evaluate how well certain efforts are working. For example, an international manufacturer of precision electronic equipment wanted us to determine how well their efforts at continuous quality improvement were taking. They were concerned because they were competing for the Malcolm Baldrige Award for Quality, a massive commitment.

This company, like many others, was vying for the award because their customers, such as Boeing and Motorola, demanded that they do it. In the leadership ranks, we saw differing degrees of enthusiasm for this effort.

We found that some teams were fired up about winning the award, others were not. In some areas of the company, people seized the opportunity to make a difference. They were productive and their morale was high. In other areas, the talk about winning the Baldrige Award was frustrating and actually resulted in cynicism and lower morale.

Always we were able to look up the organizational chart and find a senior manager who was either committed or not committed to the process. In every single case, the manager's attitude was reflected in the attitude of the team.

CASCADING MUST BE AN UNBROKEN CHAIN.   Each member of your management team must carry the banner and give airtime to the Vision Statement for the cascading process to work properly. If there is someone on board who is not leading and doesn't understand or believe in the vision, you will lose whatever span of control that person represents. This underscores the discussion in Chapter 4. You must win over *all* your managers if the process is to work.

The cascading process cannot be implemented faster than your managers are ready to move.

Natural Law 3: You Can't Walk Faster Than One Step at a Time

Seniors should not begin communicating the Vision Statement down the ranks until they understand and embrace it. Middle managers, by the same token, must understand the vision and be committed to it before they talk to their

direct reports. It is also essential that frontline supervisors understand the vision fully before going to their
workers, because it is there that results must be achieved.

Ultimately, you want to accomplish all this from a distance. If you are a CEO or a senior manager, recognize
that you can implement your vision only through the management team you employ. If you are a team leader, you
will be closer to the front line and may be able to teach
and lead directly.

The most critical mistake we see during this process is
seniors moving directly to the front line and making
proclamations about values, behavior, and culture before
the frontline management team is ready to build that culture. The most this can produce is short-term enthusiasm.
In the long run, it will actually have a detrimental effect.
If the frontline supervisors are not ready to unleash authority in the proper way, unfulfilled promises will undermine management's credibility, creating one of the gaps
we talked about in Chapter 5.

Success, in this context, can never be a guerrilla effort.
Culture cannot be built from the bottom up. Success will
happen only when each management level makes itself
ready to pass the baton down, and so on, until the entire
work force shares a culture founded on the new vision.

LEADERSHIP ACTION PLAN
CASCADING VISION OUT TO THE FRONT LINES

PURPOSE OF THIS ACTION PLAN

To share your team's Vision Statement with every member of your company and create unified commitment to the Mission Statement and Guiding Principles.

OVERVIEW OF THIS WORK SESSION

Cascading involves each manager sitting down with his or her immediate team and having a series of meetings. These meetings are made up of four steps, which we will discuss in detail in the following pages:

- Teams discuss and commit to the Mission Statement and Glossary.
- Teams discuss and commit to the Guiding Principles.
- Teams suggest changes to the Vision Statement (Mission Statement, Glossary, and Guiding Principles).
- Teams develop their own team-specific Mission Statement.

WHO SHOULD LEAD THESE CASCADING MEETINGS?

Managers should lead these meetings themselves. Don't use a facilitator. It is important for the teams to hear about the Mission Statement and Guiding Principles directly from their manager. This means each manager needs to be prepared. Managers must understand the Vision Statement and be committed to making it a reality.

The leader's goal in these meetings is to promote discussions among the staff. You should stay out of the discussions as much as possible. Talk only as much as necessary to get the staff involved. That means you will self-disclose, give examples, and talk about what the mission and Guiding Principles mean to you. Make sure, however, that by the end of the discussion meeting, your staff has carried the majority of the conversation.

CASCADING VISION: ONE STEP AT A TIME

Cascading is a top-down process that can proceed only through one successive layer of the organization at a time. For example, if the Vision Statement was created by a CEO and his or her direct reports, the next people to cascade the completed Vision Statement would be the CEO's direct reports. Each of them would meet with their respective teams for the cascading meetings described in this action plan. If the people attending these meetings are themselves managers with their own teams, they do not proceed to cascade the vision until they themselves have been through the entire cascading process with their own manager.

The meeting described here is designed to give everyone on your team the opportunity to understand and commit to the Vision Statement. You are encouraged to tailor this guide to the needs of your work group.

These guidelines may represent several short meetings or one or two long ones. Your pace is up to you and the progress of your team.

Step 1: Teams Discuss and Commit to the Mission Statement and Glossary

- Establish the purpose of this portion of the meeting: to examine, understand, and commit to the mission of the company.

- Request full participation. This should be an honest, no-holds-barred discussion reflecting all the opinions of the team.

- Lead a discussion on the importance of having a Mission Statement in the company. Using a flip chart, list reasons a corporate mission might be important to the people in the organization.

- Distribute copies of the draft of the company's Mission Statement. Read it with the group and ask for their reactions.

- Discuss how this mission applies to the work of your team.

- Discuss with your team where the company is currently living up to the Mission Statement and where gaps exist between the mission and the current reality within the company.

Step 2: Teams Discuss and Commit to the Guiding Principles

- Establish the purpose of this part of the meeting: to examine the Guiding Principles of the company.

- Define Guiding Principles as the values that should guide the decisions and actions of each person. They help create the company's culture and coordinate company-wide efforts.

- Distribute copies of the draft of the company's Guiding Principles. Point out *how* accomplishing the company's mission will determine its overall success.

- Discuss each principle separately. Ask your team:

  How do these principles apply to them personally?

  How do these principles affect the interactions of the people on the team? With the customer? How do they affect the service levels provided by the team?

What type of teamwork is necessary to serve the customers in the spirit described by the principles?

• Discuss how the principles can be used as a guide for solving various technical problems your team might encounter.

• These discussions may take several meetings. Don't move on to the next Guiding Principle until the one before you has been fully discussed.

Step 3: Teams Suggest Changes to the Vision Statement (Mission Statement, Glossary, and Guiding Principles)

• Explain that the current Vision Statement is only a draft. Part of the purpose of your meetings is to elicit suggestions for changes.

• Ask your team: How can the Mission Statement and the Guiding Principles be written more clearly? Are there any concepts or values that should be added or deleted?

• Stress that the team's suggestions will be studied on an individual basis by the senior team before it completes the final version of the Vision Statement. Provide a specific date when they can expect the final version to be announced.

Step 4: Teams Develop Their Own Team-Specific Mission Statement

• Establish the purpose of this part of the meeting: to create a Mission Statement that is unique to your team. This should encompass only the specific goals and purpose of the team.

- Begin with the question "How does the team contribute to the overall accomplishment of the company's mission?"

- Use flip charts. Ask your team to brainstorm the four questions a Mission Statement should address: Who are we? What do we do? For whom? Why?

- Once you have the answers written down, ask the team to rank them in order of importance. With a colored pen, highlight those chosen as more important. These will be included in the team's Mission Statement.

- Work with your team to include these answers in draft Mission Statements they are to write. Often it is helpful to break the team into groups of two or three people and ask each group to write its own Mission Statement. When everyone is finished, have the team, as a whole, discuss each draft. The goal is to combine the strengths of each draft into a single Mission Statement. You may wish to break away for a day or two to give everyone time to think about it.

- Don't worry if the process seems laborious. Writing Mission Statements can be time consuming. The consensus you reach through this process is well worth it, however.

- Reach a consensus and complete the final Mission Statement. Make sure everybody supports the wording and the concepts represented. It is imperative that you make it clear to all the team members that this is *their* statement of purpose, not just yours. They must be inspired by it and committed to it.

- Take some time to discuss where the team is accomplishing the mission and where it is falling short. Encourage the team to discuss the changes that could be made to close any gaps between the goals and values of the Vision Statement and the current reality within the team.

Tips for Successful Cascading Meetings

Don't Rush These Meetings

They can require weeks or even months. It takes time for
people to examine the Mission Statement and determine
how they feel about it and how they think it can be improved. It also takes time for them to absorb the Guiding
Principles and apply them in their daily working relationships.

Do not attempt to hurry this process. Remember, this is
a major change for everybody in the company. Let it sink
in, even if it takes six weeks or more. In fact, the situation
to be concerned about is when the process takes almost no
time at all. That suggests people aren't taking it seriously
or aren't bothering to discuss it.

The Process Depends on the Keystone

Webster's defines *keystone* as "the piece at the crown of an
arch that holds the other pieces in place." Without it, the
entire structure collapses in a heap. In a real sense, managers are the keystones to implementing the vision in the
teams they lead. Without the manager's full commitment
and support, the cascading process will fall apart.

If this idea seems to be a recurring theme in this book,
it is because we feel it is the gravest danger to the entire
vision process. We feel this way because, unfortunately,
we've witnessed it on a number of occasions.

One of the more graphic examples came recently when
we were asked to work with a large Eastern bank to determine how well its Vision Statement had taken throughout
the organization. It had been in place about nine months
before we arrived. The organization itself was in a state of
change even before it implemented the Vision Statement.

The primary bank had just acquired several competitors and the assimilation process was under way.

The senior management team had introduced a Vision Statement in order to build a common culture that would unite the new corporation. As you might expect, trying to forge one culture from what had been several different companies wasn't easy. But the leadership had the wisdom to know it was the only way for the new corporation to succeed. The challenge for them wasn't what to do, but how to do it.

What we found, nine months after they had completed the Vision Statement process, was that in some teams it had worked wonders, while in others it had no effect or an adverse one.

Our Second Natural Law of Organizations was plainly at work here. We found that the managers made all the difference. In some teams, the managers had simply passed around a memo stating: "These are our mission and values." They were never discussed by the team and never even mentioned again. Even worse, leadership failed to live up to the values it was proclaiming.

As you might expect, on these teams we found workers who had no faith in the organization. Many said they were openly seeking jobs with other corporations. They were disgusted and even angry at the company over the cavalier manner in which their managers had handled the cascading process. The managers were exposed as hypocrites. The frontline workers were especially insulted by the memos.

One said: "I just filed our company's culture memo in the trash. It's where it belongs." It wasn't exactly the attitude the senior management had hoped to inspire.

In other teams, however, the process was a smashing success. These teams, without exception, had taken weeks to discuss the Vision Statement. They were led by managers who took the process seriously. Their confidence and commitment to the Vision Statement was contagious. The individuals on the teams expressed enthusiasm, and a pride in and loyalty to the recently expanded corporation. They were optimistic about the future.

In one section of the company, the vice presidents had even filled in for the frontline workers waiting on customers on "teller row" for an hour every day—for weeks— so the tellers would have time to meet and discuss the Vision Statement. The effort had an enormously positive effect on the entire section. The frontline workers' morale was sky-high. They believed in the values expressed in the Vision Statement, in no small part because it was obvious that the managers were willing to live by them. We found that the Vision Statement values had already become the guidelines by which they made decisions and conducted their relationships.

The result? Within 18 months, that section boasted the lowest turnover rate and the best customer satisfaction ratings in the organization.

The key to the cascading process is capturing the hearts and minds of the managers.

7

LEADERSHIP
AFTER CASCADING

Cascading the vision throughout the organization is an exciting and dynamic process. But giving the vision airtime is just the beginning. Now you have to prove that you mean it. Seize the opportunity to build trust and belief in the vision by immediately translating it into daily action. This period after cascading is a crucial test of your leadership abilities, because building trust is vital to your organization's future.

CARPE DIEM! (SEIZE THE DAY!)

Once you have shared the Vision Statement with your employees, you have a finite period of time to demonstrate your sincerity. During this time, you must actively and visibly translate that vision into reality. When you succeed, you will reap rich rewards. There will never be a time when people are more receptive to the vision.

During the cascading process, you made a compelling promise of empowerment and continuous improvement of quality. At this point, you will definitely have everyone's attention. Your staff will be watching carefully to see whether you mean what you say. This is a critical period. When you show them that you are worthy of their trust, you will win their hearts and minds. The company will come alive with a greater force and vitality than it has ever shown before. It will launch itself down the path toward the astonishing productivity gains needed to become a world-class competitor.

Conversely, however, if you fail to act—if you fail to seize the day—you will miss an opportunity you may never have again. Once this opportunity passes, no amount of promises or hard work will succeed in turning your vision into action. People will have already decided that your promises are empty. You will have lost their trust for good.

Don't let this happen. There are commonsense, practical steps you can take to secure your employees' confidence. Your first job is to persuade people that the values and the mission truly come from your heart. They need to know that you are totally committed to fulfilling the promises the Vision Statement contains—especially those concerning empowerment and the creation of a fear-free work environment. Your workers also need to believe that the values you are espousing are your own.

Natural Law 4: Empowered
Organizations Require Trust

Remember, many of your employees have probably worked in other companies where "human potential" movements came and went like so many fads. You must prove to them that this isn't one of them.

Having made these promises, you can expect two distinct reactions. First, those who have heard promises from management before will be skeptical. Their impulse when they hear new promises is to tell each other: "All we have to do is duck. It will pass." This group needs immediate results to counter their skepticism. Be prepared to implement changes right away. Any lag time between the cascading process and the actual changes will only deepen their distrust and increase their resistance to the vision.

The other reaction you can expect is excitement. Many, who have not experienced broken promises, will be swept up in the cascading promises and will be eager to participate in the changes. This group's excitement must also be met with immediate results or it will quickly subside into incredulity. Captured, however, this enthusiasm can be a powerful force that will help create a strong belief in the mission and values and in the company itself.

This trust will also be crucial to the dismantling of the hierarchy. Whether they liked it or not, whether it quashed their creativity and productivity or not, the behavior guidance system in the traditional hierarchical structure is the only one most people have known. When you dismantle this structure, you are asking them to make a leap of faith. You are asking them to discard their old way of thinking and accept the mission and the values of the Vision Statement as their new decision-making yardsticks.

If they do not trust their leadership, your staff will not make this leap of faith. To effect this fundamental change, they must first have a clear understanding of what these new values are. Second, they must believe in them. Third, they must believe in *you* and the management team.

Trust can be compared to a light switch. It is either on or it is off. There is no middle ground. If trust is on, people will feel free to participate and add their creative intelligence to the organization. If trust is off, they will simply put in their time and search for a creative outlet outside their work.

Building trust on the heels of cascading vision is a win-or-lose proposition. There are no ties in this game, and

you don't get to play two out of three. You must win this
one. Nothing less than the organization's future is on the
line.

CREATING SAFETY

In order for the new vision to be realized, you must have
the full participation of the people in the organization.
That will transpire only if the work environment is fear-
free. Once again, you will be contending with people's
history. Most likely, some of them have worked in organizations where similar promises were made. To a large extent, those organizations remained hierarchical and
contained the seeds of fear that ultimately destroyed attempts at full participation. In simple terms, people had
been encouraged to participate in decisions, then were
criticized when they did. Now they are hearing a similar
promise: yours. You have to prove to them that they can
participate without criticism, without fear. Winning them
over won't be easy. To do so, you must build a safe work environment.

DEMONSTRATING INTEGRITY

In this context, we are defining integrity as consistency
between what you say and what you do. This relates to the
gaps we discussed earlier between the promises in the Vision Statement and the current reality in the company.
People are going to be watching management carefully to
see whether its actions are consistent with those promises.

As part of a larger reorganization, the management
team in a national retail chain had just moved their headquarters to a new state. They spent weeks developing a new

Vision Statement. The senior team was eager to move forward with the reorganization. They wanted to make plans and announce changes to the company.

When the CEO was presented with their strategy, he stopped the senior team in their tracks. He pointed out that their plan would be inconsistent with the value of participation stated in the Vision Statement. Implementing the reorganization without consulting the workers themselves would represent a lack of integrity between the Guiding Principles and management's actions.

The management team understood his point and backed up. In order to remain consistent with the Guiding Principles, they set up a series of opportunities for people to express their feelings about the proposed reorganization. In doing so, the management team came out winners in two ways. First, they gained trust by demonstrating integrity—they did what they had promised by encouraging full participation. Second, the employees helped identify issues that the management team had overlooked. The result was a better method of reorganizing the company.

LEADERSHIP ACTION PLAN

THE TASKS OF LEADERSHIP: YOUR "TO DO" LIST

PURPOSE OF THIS ACTION PLAN

To demonstrate your support of the Mission Statement
and Guiding Principles through daily leadership. This action plan lists specific actions the leaders on the team must
take to provide ongoing support of the vision that has
been shared with the team.

1. *Be a living demonstration.* The management team has
proclaimed a commitment to the Mission Statement and
Guiding Principles. Obviously, however, they must back up
that proclamation with actions. As a leader, each time you
act, consider whether your actions are consistent with the
mission and values of the Vision Statement. For example,
if your Guiding Principles call for participation, ask yourself what you can do *today* to encourage participation. If
they call for a fear-free environment, ask what you can do
today to let people know that management will not "shoot
the messenger," as is so often the case in hierarchical companies. If the mission talks about customer service, ask
what you can do *today* that will demonstrate your commitment to the customer.

In other words, the Vision Statement should be your
guide to any and all actions you take. Follow it and you
build a strong foundation of trust. Deviate from it and the
trust—and ultimately your organization—becomes a
house of cards.

It's worth noting that there are times when leaders di-
verge from their values without realizing it. For example,
we recently observed one company president who spoke at

length about the value of listening. He was quite passionate about it and exhorted every manager in his company to make listening to their employees a priority. In spite of his obvious zeal, he was one of the worst listeners we had ever observed. It wasn't that he was being deliberately insensitive. It was just that he was always so busy talking that he didn't realize he wasn't doing any listening. His blindness in this area was hurting him. The message he was sending out was that he didn't mean what he said; as a result, people lost trust.

Obviously, the point of this story is that you must be introspective and sensitive to your own actions. Ask yourself: Are they consistent with the Guiding Principles? Are they consistent every day? As a leader, you must be willing to take a long, hard look at your own actions and have the courage to change them, when warranted.

2. *Airtime.* We discussed this in the previous chapter, but it bears emphasis. The concept follows Natural Law #1: You get what you talk about. Airtime keeps the organization's attention on the vision. In the absence of regular conversations about vision, people will become absorbed by the details of their work and go back to business as usual. As a leader, you must be prepared to speak continually about vision. Constantly talking about it is another way of being a living demonstration and can help convince people that you consider the enactment of the vision an urgent priority. Airtime also pumps life and energy into the company-wide dialogue about how to translate your vision into action.

3. *Work the halls.* This is an extension of airtime. It means looking for opportunities to get out of your office and talk to the people in your company.

Be aware that this won't just happen. It takes more than good intentions. Make a conscious effort. If you don't give it a high priority, most likely it won't get done. There are far too many other demands during the day that will gobble up your time.

Many successful managers schedule wandering-around time for themselves during the day. They make it clear that they are not to be interrupted during this time. These managers know that the process serves two purposes. First, it allows them to have weekly (and sometimes daily) dialogues with their staff about vision. These discussions turn out to be beneficial for everybody involved as information and new ideas are traded back and forth. They also help deepen the staff's understanding of the Vision Statement. Equally important, the staff is able to see first-hand evidence of the managers' commitment to the process.

Here is something you might want to try. Track your time for a few weeks. What percentage of that time are you spending working the halls? We aren't talking about regular meetings here, but special time that you've set aside to talk casually with your staff about the company's vision. You may also wish to have the other managers in your organization similarly keep track of their hours. You may want to set some goals for your management team regarding the amount of time they are devoting to this activity.

Where should you talk to people? Anywhere and everywhere. Often you will be most effective dropping in on them where they work. Don't be afraid to wander around. When you meet people, ask them what they need from you to make the vision a reality. It's a question that many of them will never forget. If you ask it earnestly and listen carefully to their answers, you will make believers out of many people right then and there. It is such a bold invitation to participate and assume responsibility in the company that some will be stunned by it. Urge them to sleep on it if they can't give you an answer right away. Make it clear you'll be back to talk again. Let them know that this is the time for them to express doubts, questions, enthusiasm, or frustrations. During this process you will be building trust. Most likely, once the dialogue begins, you will

also gain some valuable insights into how the process can
be improved.

You might also consider having brown-bag lunches that
gather people together in small groups to talk about vision. This is a time when they should be urged to talk
about success stories (how they've implemented vision and
the Guiding Principles, for example). They should feel
equally free to express frustrations or suggestions on how
to make things better.

You may also want to hold one-on-one meetings (coffee
breaks, lunches, informal talks) with key people to make
sure they understand and are committed to the vision.

4. *Eliminate fear.* Continuous improvement of work
methods is the cornerstone to success in a competitive
market. At the heart of continuous improvement is employee commitment and participation. Fear is lethal to
both. It also destroys optimism, creativity, and trust. Nevertheless, fear has long been a standard component of hierarchical relationships.

In the past ten years, nearly three-quarters of the thousands of employees we have interviewed in traditional
companies acknowledged that fear is a part of their work
experience! Often this fear creates skepticism and anger.
This sarcastic reaction we once received from a candid employee is typical of many we heard: "Let me see if I've gotten this straight," the man said. "What you want me to do
is find problems in the work methods and then tell my
manager—who developed the methods in the first place.
Do I have that right?"

Obviously, the odds against improving the work methods in such an atmosphere are great. When the messenger
is shot, participation stops. Once that is understood, the
equation becomes simple. Fear stops participation; fear
equals failure.

As a leader, if you intend to empower your people, you
must be a culture builder in ways that were never required

before. Eliminating fear will be one of your greatest challenges. After you've cascaded the Vision Statement, actively ensuring safety must become one of your top priorities.

It's important to realize that fear is almost always present in a relationship where there is unequal power. This is especially true when one person has far more power and authority to say or do things that have influence over another person. No matter how hard you attempt to flatten and reorganize your company, this power differential will never be totally eliminated. There will always be some hierarchical elements left. Thus the potential for fear to fester and grow within the company will always be there. Eliminating fear and ensuring safety thus become ongoing challenges.

Some of your methods for countering fear will be structural. For example, some companies are changing to completely self-directed work teams. This takes much of the power out of the hands of top management and shares it with the team.

One of the best examples of this shift was the Boeing Company's announcement in the fall of 1991 that its new 777 jetliner was going to be built by teams. "A few years ago, we realized that if we didn't change and improve the way we go about doing our business, we wouldn't be in business 20 to 30 years downstream," Neil Standahl, vice president and 777 Division assistant general manager, told reporters. The division set up more than 200 "design-build teams," small troupes of employees from different areas, such as engineering, quality control, finance, and manufacturing. Each team concentrates on a particular facet of the aircraft. Suppliers and potential customers are often included, and information is traded freely between the teams.

"We have from the very outset tried to create an environment where there's a lot of open communication, and that means laterally and up and down, so everybody knows what's going on at all times," said Phil Condit, Boeing Commercial Airplane Group executive vice president and 777 Division general manager. "Design-build teams can talk to different people and they are all committed to the project as a whole. It works so that manufacturing feels a responsibility for the design and design feels a responsibility for the fact that's it's got to be built."

Boeing employees working on the 777 project say problems that previously would have been shuffled throughout the hierarchy now are solved quickly because team members trust each other. Lessons about self-directed teams that are being learned in the 777 project are being applied company-wide, according to Boeing managers.

Some companies have gone even further and allowed the teams to make their own evaluations and determine their own salary increases and benefits.

5. *Make sure you have no manager who continues to behave in fear-inducing ways.* The single greatest fear factor in your company is a leader who continues to manage using clout and authority. He or she is likely to be nonparticipative and punishing in disagreements. If nothing is done with this manager, you will lose everyone within his or her span of control.

If you have someone like that, do everything you can to support him or her in behaving more appropriately. This might take training, consulting, or one-on-one talks with you in which you can provide behavior feedback and goals. Make it clear that you are committed to this process and the manager must become a part of the team.

One key manager for a major company we once worked with struggled with the idea of empowering his employees. He was a West Point graduate and was locked into a hierarchical mind-set. He was a valuable manager, and the company CEO spent a great deal of time and effort to win him over. We had a number of meetings with him, and to his credit, the manager made the commitment to change. After a few months, he was finally able to support the concept of self-managed teams and the flattened organization. The break came during an emotional conversation when he admitted that the values of the company's Vision Statement were actually values he had always embraced in his family life but was never able to show at work.

Sometimes the effort fails, however. One such instance stands out clearly in our experience. One company president had a valued EVP who refused to accept the proposed changes. He simply would not tolerate the idea of an empowered work force. The president did not want to lose the EVP, so we advised that he scrap the entire Vision Statement. If the EVP wouldn't commit to it, the entire cascading process would break down and the company would be worse off than it was before.

We also made it clear that we believed the process was vital to the future of the company and ultimately more important than any one individual.

6. *Don't punish disagreement.* Safety for dissenting opinions and those offering them is critical. Without it, participation is a hopeless goal. This isn't always an easy concept to learn. For many people, it does not come naturally. You may want to have your managers receive coaching or training in how to respond to disagreement and how to actively seek out divergent opinions. They must also learn how to react when there is conflict regarding the goals or values.

However it is done, make sure that the managers get the tools they need to do this well. As the cascading process begins, there may be other people in the organization who also need coaching to learn to be productive in this new environment. Providing this coaching is another way that you show others your commitment to the process.

7. *Accept reasonable mistakes.* Identifying problems and mistakes goes to the heart of quality improvement. If people are punished for mistakes made during sincere efforts, they will begin to cover them up and refuse to make the effort. Equally troublesome, the mistakes themselves will be

hidden or minimized rather than being used as opportunities for improvement.

An example of this leadership style is Ross Perot, who asserts that his people become more valuable to him after they have made mistakes. He describes mistakes as the "tuition" he must pay in order to further the education of his people. He has learned that if people do not make mistakes, they are not trying.

Some managers have even begun to celebrate mistakes. For example, they begin their staff meetings by describing a mistake they made recently. They explain what they did, why they did it, and the circumstances surrounding the incident. More important, they talk about what they learned from the mistake and how they changed their work method to prevent it from happening again. They recognize that making mistakes can be a valuable learning tool. By talking about their own mistakes, they are able to get people to discuss their own.

8. *Translate the Vision Statement into concrete goals.* The Mission Statement and the Guiding Principles tend to be viewed initially as abstract concepts. Transform them into a working reality by establishing specific, attainable goals. For example, your Mission Statement might call, in part, for the organization to provide "world-class customer service."

After discussing what the phrase means to each person, ask your team: "What goals might be set to move the team in the direction of world-class service?" Many companies that talk about high-quality service have no way of measuring the service they provide. They have no yardstick for determining how they are doing. Have your team generate a list of short-term and long-term goals regarding the delivery of service. Short-term goals are especially important at this early stage of the process. They provide the immediate objectives that can be achieved rapidly and serve as occasions for celebration and acknowledgment.

9. *Celebrate successes.* As a leader, be constantly looking for incidents that are consistent with the company's vision. Celebrate and draw everyone's attention to them. This becomes contagious. An achievement in one area of the company that is celebrated will inspire other teams in other areas of the company to make similar advances.

Celebration also lets everyone know that you are continuing to pay attention to vision. Plan to take time out of your day—and theirs—to applaud your people for their achievements. This speaks volumes to your people about how much importance you place on their achievements. It is a powerful way to reinforce your vision and values.

10. *Motivating maxims.* Develop short catchphrases that capture the spirit of the Vision Statement (including the Mission Statement itself if it is short enough), in order to keep the mission and values alive. These aphorisms should flow right out of the Vision Statement. Use care when developing them; avoid those that sound more like an advertisement than a statement of values.

Your goal is to have these maxims become a part of the language of your company. For example, at SeaFirst Bank in Seattle, the phrase "Making banking easier here than at any other bank" is frequently thought about and talked about within the company. At Microsoft, chairman Bill Gates's maxim, "Write the software that puts a computer in every office and in every home in the nation," is a source of inspiration to people throughout the company. Give your maxims airtime. Some managers put them on posters, memos, letterheads, and pins. But most of all, they should be a part of the verbal communication in the company.

11. *Seize the "teachable moments."* Always be on the lookout for what Tom Peters calls "teachable moments." These are incidents that give you an opportunity to talk about vision in a way that reinforces it. They are the times when you can teach people how to implement vision. Sometimes a teachable moment follows something positive you've ob-

served. At other times, it will follow an action that is inconsistent with the values or mission.

For example, suppose your Guiding Principles call for those in the organization to handle disagreements in a professional manner. Chances are, however, there will be times when a disagreement turns personal and tempers flare. This is an opportunity for you to remind the antagonists that the values they have agreed to live by call for them to work out their problems openly and with respect for everyone involved. Plan to meet with them to discuss how they can handle future disputes in a calm, productive manner that is consistent with the vision.

This approach—requiring employees to solve their own problems—is very important during these teachable moments. In the weeks and months following the cascading of the vision, as the hierarchy is being dismantled, many individuals will look to you and the management team for answers. Tell them the answers lie in the Vision Statement. The decision-making guidelines they seek lie within the Mission Statement and the Guiding Principles. The most important thing you can teach them is how they can lead themselves.

One manager used to laugh at his self-managed teams when they asked him what they should do. "You don't get the joke yet, do you?" he would say. Finally, they did get the joke: They no longer had to ask him which way to go— they had the power to determine that direction for themselves. They already had the guidelines they needed, in the words of the Mission Statement and the Guiding Principles.

MANAGING
THE CHANGE

After taking the actions described in Section Two, you will have created your Vision Statement, cascaded it to the front lines, and begun to win people's trust by example. What lies ahead is the challenge of actually making the changes in the organization that are called for in the Vision Statement. Chief among them is relocation of authority to the people in your organization, building teamwork, and overcoming your organization's natural resistance to change.

This process won't happen overnight. It may take weeks, months, or even years. Don't let this deter you. For every challenge met along the way, there is a corresponding reward in the form of higher productivity, better work methods, and lower employee turnover.

As we have mentioned in the earlier chapters, there will be resistance to this transformation. Dealing with it will be one of your greatest tests as a leader. But there will be others. Teamwork and the way people relate to one another and resolve problems will need to be redefined. Managing conflict and building a fear-free, participative environment are also challenges that lie ahead.

The four chapters in this section provide action plans to help you meet these challenges.

8

MAKING THE CHANGE

The company-wide transformation you are leading not only affects the way people do their jobs, it changes the way they *think* about their jobs and perhaps even about themselves. As we have mentioned, moving away from the hierarchical mind-set will be a fundamental change for many people.

Do not underestimate the magnitude of this change. Its scope will destabilize the culture of your organization. It will cause turmoil and, at times, even chaos. Don't be alarmed. It is simply part of the process, a natural and temporary result of releasing the energy, creativity, and productivity of your people.

It is crucial, however, that you direct this chaos, that you harness this energy. Without effective leadership during this time, the company will spin furiously in place until its energy is spent. Once the forces within the organization are unleashed, they must be directed, or people will become frustrated and angry, and you will ultimately lose the trust you worked so hard to gain earlier.

To lead effectively during this time, you must understand the dynamics of the change that you have created.

Once you understand what will happen, you can anticipate and solve the problems that will arise.

The process itself presents three major sources of problems that represent significant leadership challenges. They will affect the behavior of the people in the organization—including you.

These three major challenges are:

1. Relocation of authority
2. Clash of ideas
3. Ambiguity

It is crucial that leadership meet these challenges and react positively to them. The rest of this chapter will provide you with an inside look at the three sources of problems and methods of dealing with them.

RELOCATION OF AUTHORITY

Problem 1: Managers Who Won't Let Go

Earlier we discussed why some managers will have difficulty with the relocation of authority. Some mistakenly see this shift as a diminishment of their importance to the company. Those managers who can't let go of their old style of leading will completely disrupt any attempt to establish a safe environment for the employees. If employees are encouraged to participate, then shot down for that participation, the entire process will fail. You must be vigilant during this time to ensure that the entire management team is devoting its effort to creating a safe environment.

Problem 2: The Front Line Resists Greater Authority

Some employees may also be having difficulty with the process, though for different reasons. Most likely, the majority of the people in your front line have never thought about work relationships in anything but a hierarchical way. They've spent their careers in work environments where each employee had a job description that defined and limited his or her responsibilities. Major decisions were usually left to management. Although that rigid structure often crushed creativity, motivation, and productivity, it did provide a safety net for employees. Because the boss always made the major decisions, he or she also shouldered the blame for any major mistakes. Relocating authority to frontline employees—giving them far more responsibility for making decisions than they've had in the past—will scare some people.

In fact, in our experience with companies making this change, at least half the employees we talked to admitted to being afraid of their new roles. For years, many of them had shown up at staff meetings with their yellow note pads, prepared to be told what to do. Now they were expected to participate in these meetings and in major decisions. The change took them out of their comfort zone and some had trouble dealing with their new freedoms and responsibilities. They expressed fear that it wasn't safe, that they would make mistakes or that they weren't ready. For this reason, some frontline employees may be unwilling to participate at first.

People must believe it is safe for them to participate, share ideas, disagree, and make their own decisions. Convincing people that they will not be at risk within this new system is possible only if the management team makes it safe for them. We have already discussed the importance of *every* manager being committed to the change.

Be ready to provide the training and counseling that all your employees—frontline and management—need to understand to fully embrace their new roles. This training is often crucial. Have patience during this period, but at the same time, expect to see progress.

Problem 3: An Inappropriate Focus on the Boss

For empowerment to result in improved quality and responsiveness, employees need to change their traditional focus of attention. In the top-down hierarchy, their focus is always on their immediate boss. He or she is the one they have to please to succeed in the organization. This has to change. The new focus must be on the customer. The organization of the future will require a renewed focus on serving that customer, whether those customers are external or internal to the company. This is difficult to accomplish when people are looking up, either out of fear or habit, at their boss in the hierarchy. In the new organization, each employee should have a clear line of vision between his or her work and the end user of the product or service.

CLASH OF IDEAS

Problem 1: Conflict

As the Vision Statement is implemented, a host of new challenges will arise and an equal number of decisions will have to be made. Empowerment means that the number of people making these decisions will increase significantly. As a result, the opportunity for disagreement grows almost exponentially.

This increased potential for disagreement will not be a problem if your organization already has a highly evolved method of conflict resolution. Unfortunately, many companies don't, because in the past, most decisions were handled strictly by management. The management team may have received training in conflict resolution (some have not, of course), but few frontline employees will have. As a result, many of these disagreements may degenerate into personal conflicts throughout the company.

These conflicts can undermine the network of relationships that is so crucial to the safe and participative environment you are trying to maintain. We will go into the specific steps of how to prevent this from happening in Chapter 9. For now, however, it is important to realize that this is a common hazard of the process and must be avoided.

Problem 2: Mistrust of Management

Disagreements about how to get work done will have another predictable result: mistrust of management. Because the changes are seen to have been brought about by upper management, employees will direct much of their anger and frustration at the management team. They will conclude that the management team is untrustworthy.

The president of an aerospace company implementing quality improvement and self-managed teams told us that the biggest mistake he made was to underestimate the amount of suspicion his people grew to have of him. Another CEO was so stunned by the amount of distrust his employees showed in him, he said, he was considering wearing a T-shirt to the office with the front emblazoned with the words "Stab other side."

AMBIGUITY

In this context, *ambiguity* refers to the uncertainty that people will feel as their old job descriptions are dissolved. It will take some time before their new responsibilities and opportunities come into clear focus. Moreover, additional ambiguity will occur as the traditional lines of authority are disassembled. In some ways, the resulting confusion can be the most subtle and powerful problem you will face during this time. It is imperative that you do not underestimate the amount of confusion that is likely to be generated. (Chapter 10 provides the how-to tools you will need to lead the organization through this phase.)

The list of what you don't know will be longer than the list of what you do know during this time. You—and the entire organization—need to be prepared to tolerate this period of disarray. The uncertainty that these changes create will be surprising and unacceptable to people—if they are ambushed by it. Preparing them for it beforehand, through training sessions and just talking about it with them, will take much of the surprise and fear out of this transition stage.

Define this period as a challenge to be met by everyone. You and your organization will be breaking new ground and you won't necessarily know what you are doing every step of the way. It's important for the management team to realize that for a temporary period they will not have a road map to follow. There will be times when they are making it up as they go. During this time, the only guidelines they will have will be the concepts and values of the Vision Statement.

An organization can develop needed flexibility during this period by being tolerant of ambiguity. The leadership must not only be tolerant of ambiguity, it must make it clear to the front line that this uncertainty is simply part of the process. If the management team is not actively reassuring employees during this time, the ambiguity can do severe damage. Stress levels rise, conflicts can rage out of control, and ultimately the management team will suffer a complete loss of trust.

Breaking up the hierarchy and relocating authority is analogous to having a baby. Of all the phases of the process, this is the most difficult and painful. There will be lots of sleepless nights and thankless work.

THE CHANGE–EFFORT CURVE

Take heart. There is light at the end of the tunnel. Making a cultural change is a project that follows a predictable course. In the January 1989 issue of *Training* magazine, Clay Carr graphed the effort over the time it takes to make a cultural change. As you progress from developing and cascading your Vision Statement to its final implementation, your effort will most likely resemble the following curve:

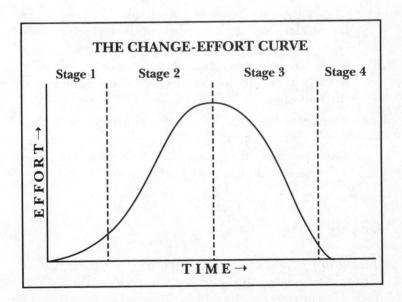

Adapted from Clay Carr, "Following Through on Change," *Training* (January 1989): 39–44.

The process can be broken into four stages:

1. *The announcement stage* usually takes place after the Vision Statement is developed and is being cascaded to the rest of the organization. This phase of the work is sometimes overdone in the form of splashy announcements and celebrations. Some companies launch their quality initiatives with a showy gala complete with buttons and balloons and political dignitaries.

2. *Implementing the vision* is where the real work begins. This is the time when the people in the organization translate the broad intent of the change into the everyday reality of how they get work done. Not only are they creating new ways of doing things, they are also unlearning the old ways. This is the time when the promises management has made must begin to come true.

3. *The change begins to take.* The effort diminishes in this stage after the change begins to take hold, yet there is considerable work to be done if the change is to become permanent. It is important to realize that even while the effort is diminishing, there is still more work being done during this time than there was in the first phase.

4. *Completing the transition.* At this point, the organization no longer must spend any conscious effort or resources making the change. The transformation into an empowered organization has been completed.

Double Duty

During this period of change, of course, people still must continue to provide the products and services they always have. It is important that the leaders and management team understand the increased effort that is expected of everyone. Not only are they continuing to produce their normal work product, they are being asked to spend time discussing a new vision and crafting a culture described by that vision.

How Long Does This Change Take?

This depends entirely on the depth of change that is being considered. If all you are doing is implementing values and getting people to think less hierarchically, it may take only a year to make the changeover. If, however, you are looking at a broad-scale transformation that includes a complete relocation of authority and continuous quality improvement, the process will usually take three to five years. Organizations doing this full-bore with serious intentions of competing for world-class recognition (such as the Malcolm Baldrige Award for Quality) usually think in terms of five-plus years.

The point is that you should go into this process with your eyes wide open, knowing what to expect. The reason this is so important is that those who lack the understanding of the effort this change requires often lose heart and fail in the process.

Why Change Fails

Most failures in the process occur because of one of the following three reasons:

1. *The importance of Stage 1 is overestimated.* This is a mistake made by the management team. There is a tendency for some managers to believe that once they have developed the Vision Statement and announced it with great fanfare to the organization, they have accomplished the change. They make the mistake of believing their role in this change is now

over, that it is now up to the rank-and-file employees
to complete it. As you can see on the bell-shaped effort curve, however, the management team's real
work has just begun at this stage.

2. *The effort of Stage 2 is underestimated.* As often as people
overestimate the importance of Stage 1, they underestimate the effort of Stage 2. They aren't prepared
for the amount of work that Stage 2 takes. The
process may have appeared very attractive to them
in Stage 1, with the development of the Vision Statement and all the celebrations. It soon becomes apparent in Stage 2, however, that the process requires
dedication and effort—especially since the primary
work of the company must still be done. Services still
need to be delivered and products manufactured
and sent out the door. Surprised at how difficult and
time-consuming the process is, those who aren't prepared for the effort will lose heart and abandon it.

The cascading we described in the second section
of this book can be thought of as a transition between Stage 1 and Stage 2. Management teams must
be aware that the effort does not stop following the
cascading. In fact, at that point it has really just begun in earnest. Translating the Vision Statement into
a reality is perhaps the biggest challenge the management team will face during the process and will
take the most work.

3. *Stage 3 is misunderstood.* Management teams sometimes make the mistake of letting up after Stage 2. After they cross over the hump of the effort curve,
some give in to a natural tendency to slack off. What
you must realize is that the process still requires more
effort than you put into Stage 1. During this time,
you are making the transition permanent. You are
finishing the framework that will hold the new organization together well into the future. Do not take
this stage lightly. Otherwise, all the hard work and

accomplishments of the first two stages will prove transient.

Companies that have abandoned efforts at continuous quality improvement, for example, have typically lost heart after about 18 months. They were unable to see the whole picture. If they could have, they would understand that while there was serious work left to be done, the majority of the effort was behind them.

So keep the faith—this process takes the time it takes. Much of the most difficult work will be done in Stage 2. The following two chapters will provide the tools to make this job much easier.

9

BUILDING TEAMS AND MANAGING CONFLICT

In his book *The Fifth Discipline,* business sage William Senge discusses the notion of a team IQ. He makes a telling point about the importance of cohesive teamwork. It is possible, he says, to have individuals each with an IQ of 130 grouped together on a single team that has a collective IQ of 67. The reason for the IQ drop is that these individuals do not work well together.

This occurs particularly during change. Often team members are unable to deal constructively with disagreements, instead allowing them to deteriorate into conflicts. They lack the vital interpersonal skills necessary to move the team forward. As a result, the team doesn't learn from experience and has a flawed decision-making process. The team, in effect, is less wise, less efficient, and less able to resolve conflicts than any of the individuals involved.

The converse of that equation is also true, however. Armed with the right interpersonal skills (teamwork tools), a group of individuals can solve problems and achieve goals far faster and more effectively than any single individual.

Leaders must make sure that everyone in the organization learns these skills. We have designed this chapter as a guide to help you help your people acquire these team-work tools.

Once you have cascaded the vision and are implementing the changes in earnest, you will find that one factor above all others will be critical to your success: getting people to talk to one another when they have a problem. A free-flowing dialogue allows employees to work together efficiently as a team and develop better work methods. It is also necessary in order to sustain a continuous quality improvement drive and for each employee to claim a measure of ownership of the organization's vision and goals.

In the final analysis, the most important ingredient in making the transition to the kind of successful company we described in Chapter 1 is providing people with the skills they need to talk to one another to solve problems.

We want to emphasize that it isn't enough for you or the organization just to be adequate at doing this. You must *excel* at building teamwork and resolving conflicts and impart these problem-solving skills to your employees. Your organization's future success depends on it.

WORKING TOGETHER IS AN UNNATURAL ACT

American business has long made an assumption that has sabotaged its ability to get work done at the highest levels. That assumption is that people naturally know how to work together.

After 15 years of observation, we have reluctantly come to the conclusion that working together in harmony does not come naturally for human beings. We would, of course, prefer to believe that people naturally pull together for the good of the group—but our experience tells us the opposite is more likely to be true. Give two people a piece of rope and, more often than not, they will end up pulling against each other from opposite ends.

It's important that you as a leader understand that while people can *learn* to work together, it doesn't come naturally. The management team must also understand this fact and be prepared to spend a great deal of time and effort teaching and coaching people how to work together effectively.

People bring two sets of skills to their work: technical skills and interpersonal skills. The American business culture has long prized the technical and largely ignored the interpersonal. In the new organization, both kinds of skills will be highly prized, but only those employees with well-developed interpersonal skills will succeed.

PERSONAL AND PROFESSIONAL RELATIONSHIPS

We believe that business success in the future will largely depend on relationships. Producing quality, empowering the front line, and sustaining that excellence will be a function of the relationships that are formed in the organization. We don't mean here relationships in a "stare-into-each-other's-eyes-and-get-to-*know*-each-other" sense. The workplace is not an encounter group. But we do think it's important to recognize that we have two relationships with each of our coworkers. The first is personal, the second professional. These are based on two different foundations. Personal relationships are based on our feelings. A personal relationship can range from casual acquaintanceship to a much deeper friendship. But regardless of the form, every employee has a personal relationship with every other employee he or she interacts with.

These personal relationships are very important. They are one of our key sources of satisfaction on the job. We feel better about our jobs when we like the people we work with. Sometimes you may *not* like the people you work with. Either way, our challenge is to work powerfully together.

The *professional* relationship exists for one reason only: to get a job done. We still bring feelings to this relationship, but doing the job takes top priority.

It is important to understand that these two relationships, personal and professional, are fundamentally different. *One of the biggest causes of ineffective communication and problem solving is people's confusing the two.*

Some people say personal relationships at work are paramount. Their idea is that if people can form strong personal bonds—if they really like each other—then the professional relationships will take care of themselves.

We assert that just the opposite is true. The fact is, a successful professional relationship not only gets the job done, it leaves all the room in the world for the personal relationship to flourish.

We believe that while both relationships are important, the professional relationship is key and must come first.

THE SOURCES OF CONFLICTS IN TEAMS

Teams can be formal or informal, structured or unstructured, and can come in any number of shapes and sizes. Some teams will appear on the organizational chart, others will be transient, formed when two or more people must work together to get a specific job done.

The overwhelming majority of tasks you do at work involve at least one other person. Put into that context, it is easy to understand the importance of each person developing the skills necessary to operate effectively in a team environment. In the new organization, where teamwork is essential, these skills—especially conflict resolution—are crucial.

In the past 15 years, we have talked to thousands of employees in all sizes of companies about the conflicts they face in their jobs. Inspired by the work of Ronald Fry, Irwin Rubin, and Mark Plovnick, one question we always ask is: "What is the most common source of serious conflict you face at work?"

How do you think the majority answered that question? How would you answer it?

At first, most people felt the cause of the problem was *the other person involved in the dispute.* What is the source of the conflict? "We have a personality problem," they would say, "and it's not *my* personality that is the problem." When they're in conflict, people think they know why: the other person, in one way or another, is being a jerk. The other person doesn't listen, doesn't care, or is in some other way hard to work with. Or the other person is simply incompetent.

Whatever the specific reason, one thing became clear. In the privacy of our own thoughts, we almost always blame the other person for the conflict. We *personalize* the conflict—we conclude the conflict is caused by a defect in the other person's character or competence.

Since most of us have worked with jerks before, it is easy enough to believe they are the cause of most problems. In investigating literally thousands of such conflicts, however, we agree with Fry and his colleagues. In the vast majority of cases, the conflict was caused not by a personality problem at all, *but by a disagreement over how to get the work done.*

This is a simple but enormously powerful concept. We tend to personalize most conflicts, but the truth is that they are professional in nature. Understanding that fact is the first step toward understanding the true source of the conflict itself.

Before we go further into the difference between personal and professional conflicts, we want to make it clear that we are not talking about the ability to *avoid* conflicts here. They cannot be avoided, nor should they be. They are inevitable when an organization is going through such a dramatic change as implementing a Vision Statement. But this shouldn't be a depressing thought. On the contrary, it should be a liberating one. Too often conflict is seen as failure. It isn't. Conflict is natural when people work together. The outcome of conflict can be positive or negative depending on how it is managed. Managed properly, conflict can lead to constructive results, such as a better understanding between people or a better method of production. Handled poorly, of course, it can cause serious harm.

But the most damaging conflict of all is one that is left unresolved. It will continue to surface, stealing energy from the teams and sometimes obscuring the vision and goals. While conflicts themselves do not cause failure, neglecting to resolve them can. Conflicts are most often left unresolved when they are personalized.

The Three Areas of Disagreement

It is our assertion that the vast majority of on-the-job conflicts are professional, not personal, in nature. In fact, only three major areas of disagreement account for nearly all on-the-job conflicts—and none of them has anything to do with personalities. They stem from a lack of common understanding involving the goals, roles, and procedures in the organization. Goals answer the questions "*What* are we to do? By *when?*" Roles answer the question "*Who* does what?" Procedures answer the question "*How* do we get it done?"

GOALS.   These involve the question of what each team is going to accomplish and by when. These goals should not be confused with the vision of the company. Vision is a broad statement of purpose and direction. The goals we are talking about here are specific, short-range targets. They flow out of vision in the sense that these are things the organization needs to accomplish in order to put that vision into action. But it isn't the big goals that cause conflict; usually it is disagreement over the short-term—daily or weekly—goals that causes friction.

Most of us have had the experience of being on a team that seemed to spin its wheels and go nowhere because its goals were unclear. Many organizations fail to establish clear goals. But we are human. We crave certainty. We make individual assumptions about what those goals should be. With each person making these assumptions separately, however, they are bound to differ, and those differences breed conflict. If that conflict is not seen as a professional disagreement that is based on ambiguous goals, it becomes personalized. What began as a common, but separate, attempt to define goals often ends up being defined as a personality conflict.

ROLES. The second major area of conflict involves the definition of roles. In the new organization, an often-asked question will be: "Who does what on this team and how do we make decisions?" As the well-defined hierarchy is dismantled, more of these types of questions regarding roles will arise. People will be working in teams where roles are far less clearly defined than ever before. Within this ambiguity, there is obviously a great deal of room for disagreement. Two people might disagree about each other's role, or they might disagree about the role of a third party.

As we will see in the next chapter, the question of who *decides* what is one of the most frequent sources of conflict.

As with the conflicts over goals, the conflicts created by role ambiguity usually become personalized—unless each person fully understands that the real source of the problem is lack of clarity about roles, not individual personalities.

PROCEDURES. These conflicts involve *how* work is done.
The room for ambiguity regarding procedures is as great
as it is with goals and roles.

On the surface, it often appears that most procedures in
a given organization—everything from procuring paper
clips to writing and presenting annual reports—are clearly
defined. When a new employee is brought on board, for
example, he or she is usually given an orientation that
consists primarily of learning the procedures. In many
cases, however, someone will frequently take the new employee aside on the first day of work and say: "Now, here's
how we *really* get work done around here."

There is a tension in most organizations between formal
and informal procedures. Moreover, it is rare when procedures between departments line up easily. The result is a
confusing array of informal and formal procedures, which
creates conflict. When these are personalized, the real reason for the disagreement—ambiguous procedures—is
obscured.

"Personality Conflicts" That Aren't

An interesting thing happens when teams follow an action plan that produces agreements about goals, roles, and
procedures. The personality conflicts that the individuals
thought they were having disappear. Most disappear because they were not there to begin with.

We once worked with a new hospital administrator who
had inherited a serious budget problem. Accordingly, he
announced a new procedure whereby all equipment pur-
chases had to be approved by him, rather than the department heads. The move stirred up a hornet's nest of
resentment. In the halls of the hospital, people were saying that he didn't trust them and that he was a turf-builder
flexing his muscles. They also questioned his abilities. Ultimately, the rap on him became even more savage: "He

doesn't care about good medicine. He cares more about the bottom line than he does treating patients."

Within a week, he had acquired the reputation of being a power-oriented penny pincher who didn't know what he was doing. We knew this man and knew that none of those characterizations were true. He came into the organization knowing that it had a budget problem, and he was simply trying to solve that problem. But because he hadn't told anyone why he was changing the procedure, they did not understand that he had the same goals as the rest of the hospital management team. The result was a misunderstanding that created a conflict, which was immediately personalized. It caused a rift that took months to heal.

To avoid these problems, it is vital that organization leaders stress to everyone in the organization that finding the real source of conflict is a top priority. Management and team members should understand that this is a skill to be learned and practiced, every day. It must be emphasized to the employees that blaming conflicts on "personality differences" is no longer acceptable.

PERSONAL VS. PROFESSIONAL.   Every employee in conflict should ask himself or herself, "Is this a professional disagreement, or am I making it personal?" This question should be asked during every disagreement.

As a leader, knowing which side of the line you are on is perhaps the most important skill that influences your effectiveness as a communicator. Separating personal from professional conflicts is a mental discipline that must become habit. Your willingness to do this will reveal how committed you are to building professionalism within the new organization.

The cost of personalizing conflict is great. Most often, it leaves us angry and frustrated. If it occurs frequently, it can undermine job satisfaction. If it continues unabated, it can ruin our productivity. It can spill over into our private lives, causing sleepless nights and even medical problems.

On the job, it makes building teamwork and solving problems impossible. It destroys the free flow of communication. With emotions running high, the chances of two people in conflict working together effectively are almost zero. Even if they don't express their anger outwardly, it will show in their demeanor and attitude. In most cases, those who believe they have a personality conflict will avoid each other, ending all hope of a productive relationship.

Silence sustains these problems, keeping them alive and often nurturing them into monsters. Hidden away, they can become secret destroyers, damaging relationships and morale. They can fester to a point where the person explodes with rage, causing even greater harm.

Understanding the real source of conflicts is an ongoing challenge that must be met by all team members if the team is to succeed. To reach agreements, which will allow the team to go forward, there must be communication on a professional level. Everyone should understand that disagreements are OK, as long as they are professional, not personal.

In the best possible world, we would enjoy everyone we worked with, but the fact is, liking another person is not a prerequisite to building a powerful and effective professional relationship with him or her. At times we all must deal with someone who is arrogant, or selfish, or who doesn't listen. Sometimes the other person really *is* behaving like a jerk. But it doesn't matter. It really doesn't matter. These personal characteristics may be a minor annoyance, but in the end, we still must make the same agreements with them to reach our mutual goals. As long as we can arrive at a shared definition of goals, roles, and procedures, personalities shouldn't play a major part in getting the work done.

A Question of Velocity

Today's marketplace calls for speed. The measure of the success of your team will be how fast it identifies, addresses, and resolves the conflicts and challenges it confronts. Every time a conflict becomes personalized or communication breaks down, it slows down that team and, therefore, the entire organization. To achieve full velocity, teams across the organization need to have a mutual understanding of goals, roles, and procedures. Each individual must be able to stay professional during conflicts and seek a positive solution.

We recently worked with employees of a bank that was acquired by a second bank. The employees were angry and frustrated by the takeover. They didn't know what was expected of them, and rumors spread like wildfire. Productivity fell off dramatically. The new bank faced a crisis. At a meeting attended by the disgruntled employees, once the rumors were dispelled we determined the root of their frustration was the ambiguity they felt about their goals, roles, and procedures. We urged them to take their questions to their new supervisors and ask for clarification. A series of meetings ensued and mutual definitions were agreed upon. Once that was done, the bank employees began functioning as a productive team once again and their anger evaporated.

LEADERSHIP ACTION PLAN
UNDERSTANDING CONFLICT

PURPOSE OF THIS ACTION PLAN

To develop a deeper understanding of the concept and experience of personalizing issues and lay the foundation for the team-building exercises in the next action plan.

WHO SHOULD ATTEND THESE SESSIONS?

The concepts discussed in this chapter and the next are useful to any group needing to work together. This session and the next chapter's session are designed to be used as a unit. They are recommended for intact work groups, such as departments, which work together on a daily basis. They are also useful for cross-functional teams or any other group of people who need to work with each other.

WHO SHOULD LEAD THESE SESSIONS?

Anyone may lead these sessions. It can be the identified team leader, someone on the team, or an internal resource person chosen for his or her facilitation skills.

ALLOW AMPLE TIME FOR THESE SESSIONS

The sessions associated with this action plan should last 30 to 60 minutes. They should continue longer if productive.

GUIDELINES FOR CONDUCTING THIS SESSION

Take care of the details

- Meet in a quiet room away from the distractions of the normal workday.
- Allow no interruptions. This means no phone calls, pagers, or people coming in to ask questions.
- Assign all team members to read this chapter before discussing the questions.
- Stay attentive. Side conversations will divert everyone's attention. Urge the team to support one another by giving this action plan their full energy and attention.

Lead discussions of the following questions:

- Why do we put off having important conversations about methods of getting the job done?
- What predictions do we make that stop us from starting these conversations?
- What is the role of fear?
- What about the desire to appear capable and not make a mistake?
- Does it make a difference if the other person is a manager with more authority than you have? Why?
- What about people from different departments or disciplines? How does that affect people's willingness to have conversations?
- Discuss examples of unresolved problems in teamwork that have diminished the efforts of the team. What was the ultimate impact on the customer and on the team?
- Discuss examples of any minor issues that were avoided, only to erupt into a larger and more damaging problem.

- Remember: This is not the time to solve these problems. The questions are designed to remind everyone that unaddressed issues are too costly to ignore. During the next session, you will work together creating an "issues list" and an action plan for resolving these problems.

10

RELOCATING AUTHORITY AND BUILDING PARTICIPATION

Recently, Japanese industrial tycoon Konosuke Matsushita had some provocative words for American businesspeople. You are in an economic war with the East and you are going to lose, he said. The reason you are going to lose is in your head. You think it is management's job to make decisions and the employee's job to implement them. And the problem, he said, is that you are convinced deep inside this is the correct way to run a business.

In the East, however, Matsushita continued, we believe that the marketplace is a dangerous place to be. In order to survive, we know that we must mobilize the creative intelligence of every single person who works for us.

Frankly, we do not agree with Matsushita's prediction that American business will lose the "war." Many signs indicate that we are willing to change to meet the challenges of global competition. But to argue that point is to lose his vital message: *In order to survive, we know that we must rely on the creative intelligence of every single person who works for us.* This concept lies at the heart of the new organization. Its practical application takes the form of the relocation of authority and building 100 percent participation in the organization.

Philosophically, this relocation of authority reflects the recognition that the traditional top-down decision-making process has failed. In the world market—and, increasingly, against domestic competition—the hierarchical structure's ability to deliver the quality of services and products required to survive has fallen short.

Once leaders understand that these old structures— these lumbering dinosaurs—must be replaced by a method of frontline decision making, there is only one basic area of questions left.

What is the process? How do you increase the individual employee's role in determining what work gets done? Ultimately, how do you relocate the authority to determine who will make decisions and when?

These questions aren't as difficult to answer as they might seem. First, leaders must understand that 100 percent employee participation refers to decision making. Everyone in the organization must play an expanded role in the decision-making process.

There are only three possible roles a team member can play. All three must be understood by all team members, because at any given time they may play any one of the three: (1) the decision-maker(s); (2) those consulted before a decision is made; (3) those informed after a decision is made. People can change roles from decision to decision, but it is vital that they *always* understand what their role is to be when any given decision is to be made.

"D": THE DECISION-MAKING FUNCTION

The person—or persons—who has the decision-making authority over the particular problem at hand is said to have the "D." The decision-making authority comes from management, and it may change from project to project.

It is imperative that who has the "D" be clear within each team, especially during complex projects involving multiple team members and multiple teams. This is true for all phases of the project, step by step, decision by decision. Clarity on who has the "D" requires constant communication between team members and, when necessary, between teams.

This step is often overlooked. Either the manager thinks it is obvious who has it, or perhaps it just doesn't occur to him or her to spell it out. However it happens, if nobody is sure who is to make the decisions, the work process will slow down. Faced with such ambiguity, team members will usually do one of two things. Some will make their own assumptions about who has the "D." More often than not, they will each come to different conclusions, which will inevitably lead to conflict. Others will revert to the company's old methods of decision making and automatically bump the decision back up the hierarchical ladder. The result in either case will be the loss of valuable time and effort.

Any ambiguity about who has the "D" can quickly lead to misunderstandings that frequently become personalized. Recently we encountered a good example of this problem. We were working with the CEO of a large manufacturing firm who expressed to us a strong dissatisfaction with his senior staff. He was especially annoyed that the staff seemed reluctant to make any decisions that were "risky." Any time a hard decision had to be made, the staff would pass the buck on to him. As a result, his workload was increasing daily. Whereas his staff left the office at 5 P.M., he often didn't leave until hours later. The situation left him tired, angry, and short-tempered.

In expressing his wrath over the situation to us, he slammed his fist on the table and raged, "Why do they have to be such wimps!"

That was his explanation for the conflict: wimpiness. He felt his top people didn't make decisions because they had no courage. In no uncertain terms he had personalized the conflict.

His staff, on the other hand, knew he was mad at them but they didn't know why. They felt they were performing to the best of their ability. They thought they were doing the right thing by passing on the difficult decisions to him. They acted that way because he had never clearly delegated authority to them. *He had never told them that they had the "D"!*

We pointed that out to him and he began to understand that the problem wasn't "wimpiness" at all, but his own failure to clearly communicate roles and procedures to his staff. To rectify the problem, he went to the post office and bought a roll of bulk mail stickers with large red "D's" stenciled on them. After that, if a memo came to him asking for a decision from someone who should have made it, he would slap a red "D" on it and send it back to the author of the memo. Sometimes staff members would leave his office with a "D" on their wrist. It wasn't long before the members of his senior staff came to understand exactly when they had the "D" and were expected to solve the problem themselves.

In the space of two weeks, he accomplished what months of criticizing their personalities had not. He was not able to begin to resolve his problem until he began making clearer distinctions about who had the "D." His new leadership motto became "Better living through clarity."

Sharing the "D"

Sometimes the "D" is shared by two or more people and, sometimes, by the entire team. In the latter case, the team members may need to reach consensus on a decision before action can be taken. If so, the team needs a procedure which ensures that the necessary people get involved and that the decision is reached in a timely manner.

The benefits of a consensus decision are that everyone involved with that decision is able to express his or her point of view and therefore the decision will most likely be the best one possible. Also, since the decision is a mutual one, its implementation is likely to be supported by the entire team.

The risk of consensus decision making is that it lacks speed. If nobody can leave the room until a consensus is reached, any person can stop the action. And as we have noted, in today's marketplace, speed and responsiveness are essential. Therefore, it is often necessary for companies to assign the "D" to one or two people. But you must not let this stifle participation.

Those on the team who don't have the "D" have another important role to play. They can *consult* on the decision before it is made. If they are not consulted, they will be informed after.

"C": THE CONSULTING FUNCTION

Those with the "C" do not have the authority to make a particular decision. Their role is to express their opinion before the decision is made. Through getting all members involved by increasing their capacity to consult, the team's IQ can be increased. Ultimately, it is the group's ability to allow everyone to express an opinion—without anyone taking it personally—that helps the group toward its best decisions. The best decisions are based on dissenting opinions, that is, an open discussion and examination of differing points of view.

Another benefit of expanding consultations is that people are more likely to support decisions when they have a role in making that decision. Those who feel they had something to offer, but were not consulted, may harbor some resentment toward the decision, even if they agree with it. The consulting role gives each team member a part to play in the process. As a result of the open discussion that examines issues, people are far more likely to understand the rationale behind the decision and thus more likely to support it.

This expanded participation has a personal benefit as well as a professional one. Participation fulfills a human need we all have: to know that we can make a difference. Sharing in the decision-making process allows people to feel better about themselves and find more satisfaction and meaning in their work. The result is a more inspired and productive employee.

It is important for those playing this role to understand its parameters, however. Suppose, for example, that as a senior manager, you need to call a meeting regarding a major decision that must be made. The decision affects your team and you want to give them the opportunity to participate.

If they are not told beforehand that they will be playing a consulting, or recommending, role in this decision, and that they do not have the "D," a misunderstanding is likely.

If they don't perceive their role clearly, they will often think: "Wonderful. *We* are going to meet, *we* are going to have a discussion, then *we* are going to decide." Coming into the meeting with this expectation, they are likely to be resentful when they find they don't have the "D."

So be clear early. Let your team know they have the consulting role, and that you will not make up your mind until you have heard what they have to say.

You must also make clear to your team, however, that not every recommendation they give may be followed. There will be times when you (or the person who has the "D") will go against their advice.

People must not take that personally. They must understand that the consultant's role is important. It provides the opportunity to influence the decision maker before a decision is made. Consultants may offer a point of view, information, and recommendations in any way they see fit. However, consultants must also realize that there comes a time when attempts to persuade the decision maker must cease and the decision must be made. Once the decision is made, the team needs to go forward and act on it. At this point, the consultant's role is over. The consultants must now accept the decision and support it, even if they disagree with it.

It should be underscored continually that consultants will not always get their way. With 100 percent participation, there will always be differing points of view.

It is vital, however, that all team members playing the consultant role continue to offer their points of view, even if they are in the minority and even if the decisions frequently go against them. They must understand that even those (and sometimes *especially* those) minority views are essential to the long-term health of the company.

Increasing the "C"

As a leader, one of your challenges during this time will be to create as much consultation within the organization as possible. By that we mean every person in the organization should be participating in helping the person with the "D" make the best possible decision. Everyone, in one form or another, should be included in the decision-making loop.

Employees, operating as a team, will make smarter decisions after they have consulted with one another than they will as individuals. One man who understood this was General Douglas MacArthur during World War II. Although he always made it clear that he ultimately had the "D," he nevertheless took pains to listen to his entire staff before making a decision. Given the peculiar influence that rank has in the military on people's willingness to share their ideas, he would start by asking the opinions of the lowest-ranking person first. He would then move around the table in order of increasing rank. He made these efforts because he knew that if he heard from everyone on his team, ultimately he would make a better decision.

One executive in a large Midwestern insurance company recently wanted to underscore the importance of his team's participation as consultants during the decision-making process. He thought about it for a time, then came up with an idea. He had bright, colorful posters made and hung prominently throughout the company's headquarters. They read: "C's the opportunity."

Guidelines for Making the Consulting Role Work

MAKE SURE THE CONSULTING ROLE IS CLEARLY UNDERSTOOD. As we have mentioned, teamwork will often break down when individuals are confused about their role.

For example, without a clear understanding, a task force assigned to *study* a problem and make recommendations might often assume its role is to *solve* the problem. As a result, its members may actually design and implement an action plan. Since they were only to act as consultants, valuable time has been wasted. Moreover, when they learn of their error—which resulted from unclear instructions from management—they are likely to feel frustrated and angry and far less willing to commit 100 percent to the next project.

LISTEN TO YOUR CONSULTANTS. Sometimes managers make a pretense of participation and ask for consultation but then ignore it. We have even seen managers ask for consultation after the decision has already been made. These are dangerous deceptions which rarely work. People know when they are being duped. The result is a loss of trust and faith.

ALWAYS INFORM CONSULTANTS ABOUT DECISIONS AND THE RATIONALE FOR THOSE DECISIONS AFTER THEY ARE MADE. Failing to do that will cause frustration among the teams. The members will feel left out, almost as if they weren't asked to consult in the first place. If employees are committed to the project and to the vision, they will naturally want to know how and why a major decision was made. Telling them about the decision allows managers to thank all the team members for their efforts and to actively seek their support for the decision. This is especially important if the decision has gone against the consultants' recommendations.

A SPECIAL NOTE TO MANAGERS: BE WILLING TO NOT KNOW EVERYTHING. One of the most important skills in an organization that values participation is a willingness to accept ideas from others. Managers must understand that it is OK for them not to know all the answers. This is especially true when the manager has the "D." He or she must be able to say: "I have the 'D,' but I have no idea yet what my decision will be. I need your wisdom."

This is not a simple skill. Traditionally, managers have risen to their position by knowing the answers. In many cases, this omniscient attitude has become part of the ego structure of the manager. Over the years, his or her self-esteem can become tied to it. Obviously, these managers will have a difficult time giving up this authoritarian throne. But they must be able to do it if they are to be effective.

Other managers, while not on a power trip, will have difficulty with the temporary ambiguity of not knowing the answer right away. The ambiguity scares them and they will make decisions quickly, without waiting to go through the consulting process.

Regardless of the reason, any manager unwilling or unable to not know everything will destroy participation and ultimately decrease the productivity of the employees if he or she cannot change. It is impossible to contribute to somebody who knows everything.

"I": INFORMED AFTER THE DECISION

Once a decision is made, every team member whose work is affected by it needs to be informed about it. Sometimes management teams are in constant communication with each other during the decision-making process, then fail to follow up after the decision. This is an essential step that should not be overlooked. Whenever the decision is controversial or complex, the rationale behind it should also be explained after it is made. Doing this will accomplish several beneficial objectives.

First, it will keep everyone informed about the direction of his or her team. Second, it will show respect for that person by including him or her in the decision-making envelope. It will also properly close the decision-making loop, promote teamwork, and help the company's drive toward 100 percent participation by making everybody part of the decision-making process. Finally, it will provide information about the decision so it can be implemented properly.

The fact that there are only three roles makes conversations about decision making simple. What is needed is clarity. Each member needs to know whether he or she has the "D," the "C," or the "I."

MAKING THE RELOCATION OF AUTHORITY REAL

Understanding these three roles enables people in the organization to increase participation and begin to relocate authority. Following are steps to take to push decision making as close to the front lines as possible. This can be satisfying and exhilarating.

Organizations can break up hierarchical structures in two ways: by relocating the "D" and by greatly expanding everyone's consulting role. We'll take a closer look at both of these actions.

Relocating the "D"

The lessons of the quality revolution show that decision-making responsibilities should be given to those closest to the production of the product or service. Decisions should never be made by managers when they can be made by those who actually do the hands-on work. This is where the knowledge regarding producing or serving at world-class levels is to be found.

As a leader, ask yourself: How many decisions am I currently making that really should be made by those who are closer to the customer or service? Where is it that we need to transfer authority to the front line?

Those on the front line should ask: What decisions can we make that would speed up the work and enhance quality?

Teams are slowed down when they have to wait for decisions to be handed down from a rigid multilevel hierarchy. Simple decisions like the allocation of funds for training can sometimes take weeks when they should take minutes. Even worse is the horseshoe of authority that must be followed for decisions involving more than one department. Rather than going directly to a peer on a different team about getting something done, workers have to request a decision from their boss, who talks to his or her boss, who then deals with his or her peer. The decision making then descends down the levels of the second team until it reaches the front line again. Often the process has to come back around the horseshoe before the decision is finally passed on to the employee who initiated the question in the first place. The result is an incredible waste of time and effort.

Relocating Authority Works!

Companies across the United States and throughout the world are beginning to eliminate first-line supervisors in favor of self-managed teams, which make all the decisions traditionally made by the supervisors. This includes hiring, firing, planning the daily work calendar, and making all the daily decisions, which include production method improvements.

By 1990, 7 percent of the Fortune 1000 companies already had self-managed teams, and more than 50 percent said they intended to create them in the near future.

Some of the results of the self-managed teams are already in:

- The Kellogg Company has both traditionally organized factories and factories run by self-managed teams producing similar products. Those that are based on self-managed teams have reported 40 percent higher production levels than the traditional factories.

- The Xerox Corporation has 18 plants with self-managed teams which have reported productivity increases of 30 to 40 percent.

- Tektronix Corporation reported that one self-managed team does in three days what used to take an entire assembly line two weeks.

- General Motors reported a 40 percent productivity leap because of self-managed teams.
- Shenandoah Life, a major insurance carrier, reported that its self-managed teams are able to process 50 percent more applications and customer service requests with 10 percent fewer people.

We cannot rest on our laurels. We must continue to strive to improve all our methods of production and service in order to compete in the global marketplace. Today's challenge to American business is to build a more participative environment, relocate authority, and tap the inspirational and creative talents that every American worker possesses.

Some people question whether the American worker is up to it. Some believe the hierarchical mind-set is too entrenched, too ingrained in the American culture for these changes to be made.

We strongly believe that just the opposite is true. The examples we cited earlier in this chapter and elsewhere in this book are proof that American workers are not only capable of this change, but will flourish in its empowering environment.

LEADERSHIP ACTION PLAN

THE ISSUES LIST:
BUILDING TEAMS AND PARTICIPATION

PURPOSE OF THIS ACTION PLAN

To build better teamwork, increase participation, and develop an Issues List that becomes an ongoing technique for team development.

OVERVIEW OF THIS WORK SESSION

Teams and individuals will:

- Discuss conflicts and apply the language of goals, roles, and procedures to diagnose the source of conflicts that may have been taken personally.
- Start an Issues List, compiling a list of issues that need to be addressed.
- Arrange these issues in order of importance and create action plans to respond to those most in need of resolution. The Issues List becomes an ongoing source for the team's monitoring of actions needed for the team's maintenance.

BEFORE THIS SESSION

Make sure that everyone on the team has read Chapters 9 and 10.

LEADING THE GROUP SESSION

Step 1: Each Person Should Think of a Real Job Conflict He or She Has Had or Has Witnessed

Preferably, this will be one that is current, but they can also choose an example from a previous job.

Ask a volunteer to describe a conflict. Ask:

- Who was involved?
- How did those involved feel about it?
- How was this conflict personalized?
- How did personalizing interfere with getting the issue resolved?

Lead a group discussion.

- What is the group's reaction to this situation?
- Can this be better understood as a professional difference of opinion that has been personalized?
- Can the issue be diagnosed as a disagreement about goals, roles, and/or procedures?
- Is authority regarding decision making involved?
- What agreements need to be reached to resolve the issue?

If time allows, more volunteers can describe a conflict for discussion. Again, see how each conflict can be understood as a disagreement over goals, roles, and procedures.

Step 2: Ask Your Team How They Would Benefit By Using the Concepts and Language of Goals, Roles, and Procedures

- Would it become easier for them to have conversations regarding potential conflicts? If so, why?

- In what ways would they benefit? How about the customer? Quality?

Step 3: Ask Them Where the Opportunities Are to Enhance Participation in Decision Making

- Where do they need greater clarity in decision-making roles?
- Where can team members take on greater authority?
- Where would team members like to be consulted more? By whom?

Step 4: Start an Issues List

An issue in this context is any problem interfering with the delivery of the products or services. This can include any situation in which goals, roles, and procedures are unclear or conflict. Most issues are not problems. They are the relatively minor glitches or improvement opportunities that affect service and teamwork.

Working with a flip chart:

- List any issues that are currently causing concern to the group: problems interfering with teamwork, customer service, quality, and so on.
- List freely until the group has run out of ideas.
- Review the list, making sure that issues have been described using the language of goals, roles, procedures, and decision making.

Step 5: Have the Team List These Issues in Order of Importance and Have Them Discuss Their Reasoning

This list should now be prioritized on the basis of impact on getting the job done.

Step 6: Have the Team Place the Top Three Items in Order of Importance

This may take some time as the team discusses which issues have the greatest effect and offer the greatest opportunity for gains if resolved.

Step 7: Create An Action Plan for Dealing with Those Three Items

This plan should identify *what* is going to get done, *who* will be involved, and *by when* it will be accomplished.

Some plans will identify things that can be done by team members directly. Others will be issues requiring management attention. Be sure to identify who needs to be contacted and who will make the contact.

Step 8: Have the Issues List Typed and Distributed to Team Members

Step 9: Keep the Issues List Active As a Self-Management Tool

The team should discuss it on a regular basis. Remove issues that are no longer current. Add new ones as they appear and create new action plans.

*Sample Issues List (generated by a
corporate information systems division)*

1. Department managers' authority is poorly defined.
2. We have no consistent project methodology.
3. User groups (corporate departments we serve) are not being adequately consulted on the design of systems.

4. We have no way to establish the priorities of projects.

5. Goal conflicts among our departments.

6. User groups complain that we don't understand their businesses.

7. User groups are hiring their own programmers due to our slow response time.

11

THE THREE STAGES OF CHANGE

Building the new organization sets enormous changes in motion. If the dynamics of change are not understood by everybody in the organization, change can be destabilizing and disruptive.

The changes will take place on an organizational level as teams adjust to new situations. They will also take place on a personal level as individuals cope with their own emotional responses to their evolving roles.

These changes, like all major life changes, carry with them a potentially explosive mix of uncertainty and doubt. However, they also contain the promise of increased personal inspiration and creativity, as well as greatly accelerated organizational productivity. This is a crucial stage in implementing your vision. Its success or failure hangs in the balance.

In order to lead your business through this difficult period, you must understand the effects that change will have on both the organization and individuals. You absolutely cannot afford to be blindsided by the disruptions resulting from organizational change.

This chapter provides a change model that breaks down the predictable reactions to change into three stages. It also provides a step-by-step method to teach your teams how to turn change into a positive and productive experience.

A Model of Personal Change

Some years ago, two of the authors of this book decided to change jobs and geography. We uprooted our families and moved from the Midwest to the Pacific Northwest. The result was the biggest life change either one of us had ever experienced. A downturn in the economy slowed our initial business start-up, which led to uncertainty and apprehension. Suddenly, we found we missed the safe and secure lifestyle we had left. As time went on, we experienced acute confusion and anxiety and we spent many days and nights wondering whether we had done the right thing.

It was during this time that we became acquainted with a book by William Bridges, called *Transitions: Making Sense of Life's Changes*. We were amazed by Bridges's insights into how change affects people in their personal lives. He described with remarkable accuracy the process we were experiencing. After reading it, we felt we had a better understanding that what we were going through was part of a normal process. Once we understood the process, much of our earlier confusion and anxieties disappeared. We also found that after we made some adaptations, Bridges's model of personal change also works as an excellent model for organizational change.

Ensure that every manager in your organization understands this change model. This knowledge will be essential in the new organization.

The beauty of this model is in its clear, simple logic. It is not difficult to understand, yet it contains a powerful tool for leading during change. The model outlines three stages of change: the Ending, the Middle Zone, and the New Beginning.

The Ending

Although it is the vision of the New Beginning that motivates most changes, the first phase of any change is an ending. In order for something to be born, something old has to end or change in some way. What often throws people, however, is that along with this ending comes a feeling of loss.

This sense of loss, which at times can be acute, often takes us by surprise. This is especially true when we have initiated change for positive reasons but find ourselves saddened, looking back, and missing what used to be. The pain of the Ending can sometimes be strong enough to undermine our resolve to see the change through.

We begin to think: "If the change I wanted to make was really so positive, I wouldn't be feeling this way." Faced with such a powerful negative emotion, we seriously question whether we have done the right thing.

Our determination to change can crumble quickly during this stage because much of our sense of self and security is derived from familiarity and constancy in our daily lives. It is that sense of familiarity that ends when a major change is made. In many cases, the Ending is accompanied by feelings of insecurity. *We should recognize this feeling as a natural part of change.* If we aren't prepared for these feelings, the change is often seen as not worth it, and we give up the effort and retreat to familiar ground.

The Middle Zone

If we survive the Ending, we arrive in the Middle Zone. This is a time marked by confusion and self-examination. The old familiar routines have been broken and the new ones aren't yet in place. It is a time of re-creating a personal vision and developing new skills to implement it. There may be a number of false starts and failed attempts as we try to discover what works and what doesn't. A common feeling expressed during this time is: "Nothing works here; I'm not sure what I'm doing." Feelings of anger, frustration, and stress are likely during the Middle Zone.

The New Beginning

In time, however, we reach the promised land—the New Beginning. The old ways are behind us and the fog of confusion of the Middle Zone begins to clear. Eventually, as we develop the new skills and routines required by the change, we begin to reestablish a foundation of the familiar. Life seems to make sense again. This stage is often accompanied by a surge of optimism. Successfully negotiating the change instills confidence in us that we can face any challenges that might lie ahead.

Be Prepared for All Three Stages

People generally initiate a change because they focus on the picture of how things will be after it has taken place. But few are prepared for the reality of the change process itself. Most are ambushed by the feeling of loss created by the Ending. Others don't survive the Middle Zone, with its confusion and destabilizing effects.

That is why this model can be so helpful. It allows people to anticipate and understand the troubling feelings they will experience during the first two stages.

The model itself creates a sense of optimism. It is encouraging to know that change has a predictable course and that we will get through the feelings of loss, confusion, and ambivalence. It is especially important to have this understanding during times of uncertainty, so we know we aren't going crazy. It lets us know that just because we experience some negative emotions during this process, we haven't made a mistake. If what we are going through can be seen as the natural part of a process, it instills confidence that we are on the right track to seeing the change through.

The model also identifies critical skills that are necessary to sustain the change. To get through the Ending, for example, we have to recognize where the feeling of loss comes from. It also points out that we need to let go of the old ways—that letting go is one of life's essential change-management skills. Those who can't let go of the old ways will have no psychological space in their lives for anything new. Driven by a fear of the loss of security, these people will have difficulty making any type of meaningful change.

Another primary skill needed during change is a high tolerance for ambiguity. Confusion, uncertainty, and some self-doubt are all part of the change process and must be ridden out. The final strength of the model is its message that we need to actively create the New Beginning. The quickest way through the confusion and uncertainty is to maintain a focus on the ultimate goal: the reason for making the change in the first place. It's important to realize, though, that the New Beginning doesn't just happen by itself. We must energetically create it. This can be done through a broad range of activities: clarifying our own personal vision, developing new technical or interpersonal skills, and, in some cases, developing an entirely new set of habits, relationships, and other ways of relating to the world.

Generally, the size and complexity of the change will determine the depth of the emotions you will feel in the

Ending and the Middle Zone, and the amount of work required to create the New Beginning.

CHANGE IN ORGANIZATIONS

Over the years, we have adapted Bridges's personal-change model to work on an organizational level. The modified three stages are a very useful way of understanding corporate change.

The Organizational Ending

To better understand the effects of Endings on people in the workplace, there are a couple of things to keep in mind.

A recent national poll found that Americans rate work as the first or second most important thing in their lives. Those who rated it number two generally ranked it just behind their family.

For most of us, much of our sense of identity, competence, and self-worth is tied to our work. Moreover, our personal and financial security depends on a stable work situation.

Despite people's financial dependence on what happens at work, most have very little control over changes there. As a result, many of us experience change at work as something that happens *to* us rather than something we initiate. We don't have the "D." Often we are thrust into the change process without even being consulted about it beforehand. It's little wonder, then, that most people have a built-in resistance to change.

When a major decision is made to reorganize a section or department, an employee's first reaction is not likely to be "This is an excellent move for our customer and for the company," but rather "How is this going to affect me? I didn't choose to make the change. I don't know much about it and I *don't* think I'm going to like it."

Endings at work are almost always perceived by employees as bad news. The greater the change and the less they know about it, the more likely they are to be concerned about it. Anything that may change their jobs is initially going to be perceived as a threat.

Obviously this does not happen with every change. But when positive changes get negative reactions, this model provides clues to understanding them.

Recently we observed a classic example of how wary employees can be of major changes involving their organization. We were working with the management of a hospital shortly after the hospital had been sold. It had been operated by a religious order before being purchased by a public organization which had its headquarters in another state.

We knew that the sale represented a New Beginning that could offer tremendous opportunities to the employees. Being part of a larger corporation meant better funding, better chances for career development, and a broader array of patient services. Nevertheless, the staff reacted to the news as if it was the announcement of the death of a close friend.

Initially, nobody at the hospital believed that the change could be positive. Their first response was a collective feeling of loss that the old way was ending. Their second response was that they were certain of only one thing: they were not going to like the new way—whatever it might be.

This resistance to change has to be recognized and dealt with by senior management. Many people will simply withdraw and refuse to do anything that puts them at further risk when they are faced with the uncertainty of a major change. If left unaddressed, this reluctance to move forward will create an organizational inertia that will slow and even stop the change process.

A corporate president whose company was undergoing a significant change remarked to us that his best people were hanging back. Once he understood the process of change, however, he was able to put their reluctance into its proper context and ultimately win them over.

When the old ways end, productivity naturally drops. People's attention is on the change and how it is going to affect them. That productivity loss can be minimized, however, by preparing people for the change before it happens. The more they understand the process of that change, the less fearful, confused, and frustrated they will be.

HOW ENDINGS AFFECT THE TRANSITION TO THE NEW ORGANIZATION.   New Beginnings are dramatic. But while they hold tremendous potential, they aren't free. People have to be willing to experience many Endings along the way toward creating the new organization. Here are some examples of the Endings this change will produce.

- Traditional hierarchical roles will be drastically altered as the top-down authority structure is flattened. Career paths will change as the number of management jobs to aspire to declines.

- Managers will revise their methods of managing. Some may have been successful for years doing it the old way, but they will still have to learn to change. They will be asked to let go of their traditional reins of authority and think of themselves more as leaders and coaches than as "bosses."

- People working on self-managed teams will no longer have the security of a tightly defined set of goals and job descriptions. They will be expected to forge their own set of responsibilities in a less defined work environment.

- People will be asked to learn how to be team players with a greater emphasis on interpersonal skills. No longer will people be able to work as Lone Rangers, minding their own business, having limited contact with their peers. People will have to learn how to work effectively with their fellow team members.

• The hierarchy, rank, titles, authoritarian attitudes, and solitary work practices will all be ending.

LEADING DURING CHANGE. Getting past these Endings will take time. It is important that you as a leader know what to expect. The anxiety, frustration, and even fear that people will feel is natural—don't take it personally. Above all, do not interpret these reactions, which at times can be intense, as evidence that you have made a mistake by instituting the change in the first place. If you know what to expect, you won't be blindsided by these reactions. Rather than second-guessing yourself when confronted with these emotions, you will realize that they are just a natural part of the process.

The Corporate Middle Zone

The Middle Zone of the transition to the new organization is marked by ambiguity. The old vision and traditional way of getting things done are ending, but the new vision and structure are only beginning to take form. People are uncertain about what their next step should be. They aren't sure, yet, how to get things done, both as individuals and as teams.

The ambiguity causes two predictable outcomes:

1. **Without information or direction, people conclude the worst.** It is natural during these times of apprehension for employees to seek or establish some sense of direction or certainty. Management must provide it through the steps we have outlined. This process includes cascading the Vision Statement,

constant discussions about goals, roles, and procedures, and through general encouragement for everyone to discuss questions and fears.

If you fail to do this, the anxiety that employees feel during the Middle Zone tears apart the trust you have worked so hard to establish earlier in the process.

A common trap for senior management in the Middle Zone is for the managers themselves to fall victim to the uncertainty. Since many of the new procedures are not yet established, some managers will delay talking to their teams until there is more certainty. But it is a grievous error to withhold information when employees most need it. The inevitable result is that people will fill the vacuum with rumors, speculation, misinformation, and distortions.

A good example of this occurred in the hospital mentioned earlier in this chapter. After the hospital was purchased by the public corporation, a senior management official from the out-of-state headquarters came to spend some time at the hospital. He understood that many of the employees were upset over the sale and he wanted to do what he could to alleviate their fears and anxieties. He did his best to be reassuring. He attempted to compliment the staff by noting that many of them had more than 10 years' experience and some had been at the hospital for their entire careers. He followed up the compliment by asking questions about the pension plan. His motivation was to ensure that those longtime employees would be cared for after they retired.

Those innocent comments sparked a rumor that raged throughout the entire organization in a matter of days: "If you have been at the hospital for more than 10 years, you will be laid off by the new owners." Soon the entire hospital was in an uproar. The employees—following a natural course—had filled the information vacuum with speculation and distortions.

2. **Conflict increases in the Middle Zone.** As individuals and teams invent methods of getting work done more efficiently, conflicts are likely. Everything is changing: the goals, roles, and procedures, as well as the entire vision of the organization. New decisions will have to be made every day. On a statistical basis alone, there are far more opportunities for disagreement. Add the inherent confusion of the Middle Zone to the mix and the potential for conflict is obvious. During this uncertain and stressful time, people personalize disagreements more than ever. Unchecked, this practice leads to a damaging breakdown in teamwork and communication.

Some managers may feel as though their roles will be diminished in the transition to the new organization. Those fears will be blown to smithereens once they understand the challenges of leading their teams through the Middle Zone.

THE LENGTH OF THE MIDDLE ZONE. How long the Middle Zone lasts is largely a factor of how well the change is being orchestrated by the senior management team. If communication is maintained, and employees as well as management know what to expect during this period, it can be as short as a few weeks. However, we've seen organizations get mired down and struggle for months without much progress. These failures inevitably result from management allowing communication to break down, rumors to go unaddressed, problems to go unsolved, and ambiguity to go unchallenged.

The goal of effective leadership is to skirt these pitfalls and to shorten the Middle Zone. It is a potentially dangerous place to be. As one company president told us: "This isn't the Middle Zone, it is the *Muddle* Zone. We are muddling around in confusion."

The change–effort curve we discussed in Chapter 8 becomes more understandable in this context. This is a far more difficult period than the initial development of the Vision Statement and the cascading process. In this Middle Zone we are spending our time and effort defining and focusing on our new goals, roles, and procedures, while at the same time trying to deal with the insecurities of abandoning the old ways.

The only way to get through this time of confusion is to create new ways of working together. There are no exact road maps that will lead you to the New Beginning. You must develop these methods as you go. As a leader, constantly encourage communication in order to tap in to the wisdom of your employees. It is their responsibility, as well as yours, to help develop these new methods. It is part of their emerging role in the new organization. Understanding even that aspect of their new role will help dispel their uncertainty and accelerate the change process.

Guidelines for Shortening—and Surviving—the Middle Zone

1. *Make sure everyone in the organization is informed about the vision and the changes taking place in the goals, roles, and procedures.* Share the information—fill the vacuum. Remember that people will be experiencing apprehension and even fear during this period. They may need to be exposed to the same information a number of times before they actually comprehend it. *It is almost impossible to overcommunicate during the Middle Zone.*

    It's important that management never assume that people have all the information they need or that if they didn't, they would ask. As we have pointed out, many people will withdraw during times of stress and management must go to them.

A few years ago we worked with a bank executive whose bank was being acquired by another. His bank was in the midst of due diligence, just before the sale was to be finalized and approved. It was an awkward and anxiety-ridden time for most of the employees, who weren't sure of their future. We asked the executive what he had done to alleviate his employees' fears. He very proudly pulled three memos from his desk that cryptically explained the acquisition. "Besides," he said, "my door is always open. I'm sure that if anyone had a question for me, they would ask."

We had already talked to people in the organization and knew how hungry they were for information. Most of them had no idea what due diligence meant or how it would affect them personally. They felt so threatened and vulnerable, however, that they withdrew rather than question this executive, who rarely talked to them anyway.

We suggested that he meet with frontline employees and answer their questions at a corporate retreat. After two hours of sitting in front of the group, he looked like the guy in the stereo ad—his hair and tie blowing back from the hurricane of questions.

"I had no idea," he said in amazement.

It was clear from the questions that people were not only confused as to what was happening with the bank, they were angry and mistrustful of management for not telling them. They resented being kept in the dark. Not informing his people cost this man dearly in trust and commitment. It also diminished the organization's productivity. Once he understood that, however, he was able to reestablish communication and begin to repair the damage.

Keeping people informed is nearly a full-time job during the Middle Zone of change. Don't underestimate either how long it will take or the importance of doing it.

2. *Be decisive.* Don't "muddle around" in the Middle Zone: make decisions to get your team through it. Some teams get stuck there because management—and they themselves—don't make the decisions necessary to move forward. It is easy to fall behind on the effort curve here.

3. *Get everyone involved in making decisions.* Actively ask people for their opinions and recommendations. Involve teams and individuals directly in creating their own goals, roles, and procedures. Give these teams and individuals the "D" whenever possible. When the "D" cannot be delegated, expand the opportunities for consultation—the exchange of information—between teams, individuals, and levels of management.

   Participation pays off. It will get the team to the New Beginning faster and it will reduce the overall level of anxiety in the organization. People feel less helpless when they are involved with engineering the changes.

4. *Be patient.* This is a stressful time. People need to feel free to talk and express their feelings. Listen to them. Make yourself available for private talks. Develop an emotionally supportive environment in which people feel they are going through this together.

5. *Be vigilant for conflict.* As we discussed earlier, teams have more than the usual number of opportunities to take disagreement personally during change. Personalized conflicts need to be identified quickly and resolved professionally. It is imperative that the team relationships survive this tense time.

6. *Educate people about change.* Expose people to the change model. Let them know, in detail, about the three stages and what they should expect in each stage. Be sure to stress the importance of communication during this time. They need to understand the change as an opportunity, not as a threat.

MAKING CHANGE CONTINUAL

Although the New Beginning marks the end of the three stages of change, it by no means marks the end of change itself in the new organization. Indeed, continual change will be the hallmark of the successful organizations of the 21st century. To stay competitive, organizations will constantly seek new ways of achieving higher levels of quality at lower prices. One of the leader's primary goals in the new organization will be to lead that search. The organization itself must be flexible enough to allow for these innovations.

So give up any hope that things will ever get back to normal. "Normal," from now on, will be a highly dynamic and inspired workplace where continual changes in goals, roles, and procedures are not only allowed but encouraged as the organization strives for productive innovation.

This means changing our relationship to change itself. Successful organizations of the future will embrace change. Managers, especially, must be willing to thrust themselves into the ambiguities that change brings. They must be able to lead their teams through the uncertainty and teach them to see change as an opportunity. This means that managers, above all, must abandon their efforts at trying to control everything.

For most of us, this requires a personal readjustment of our view of change. We have been schooled, whether consciously or unconsciously, that change is inherently bad. It is destabilizing and triggers our fears of the unknown.

In the past hundred years, businesses survived by managing in a way that assured stability and discouraged change. But the world marketplace has changed and obviously we must change with it. Organizations must develop a high velocity, and the fuel for this velocity is the ability to change. Change, managed correctly, is no longer a threat but a necessity. It is the source of improvement. Continual change is the source of continual improvement.

LEADERSHIP ACTION PLAN
UNDERSTANDING AND IMPLEMENTING CHANGE

PURPOSE OF THIS ACTION PLAN

To enable teams to apply the change model in an effort to better understand the impact of change on teams and individuals and to use that understanding to implement change more skillfully.

OVERVIEW OF THIS WORK SESSION

Team members will:

- list changes currently affecting them.
- discuss the relevance of the change model as a tool for coping with the impact of change on an individual and team level.
- identify any outstanding issues to be added to the Issues List.

BEFORE THIS SESSION

Make sure everyone on the team has read Chapter 11.

LEADING THE GROUP SESSION

Step 1: List and Discuss the Impact of Changes on the Team

Using a flip chart or blackboard, create a list of changes affecting the team.

- Ask the team to list all the changes that are currently having an impact on the team.

- Ask them to list recent changes or changes anticipated in the near future.
- Ask them to discuss the impact of these changes. How have these changes affected them as individuals? How have these changes affected the teams involved? Impact on morale? Service? Productivity? Quality? Participation? Trust? Communication?

Step 2: Apply the Change Model in Understanding These Changes

At a flip chart, write *The Ending* at the top of the page and *The Middle Zone* at about mid-page. Given all the changes they have discussed, ask the team to list effects of change that can be understood as associated with the Ending and the Middle Zone.

Step 3: Creating New Beginnings: Taking Action

On a new flip chart page, write *Creating New Beginnings*. Ask for and list responses to these questions:

- What are some of the things this team needs to do better to manage some of the changes we have discussed?
- Are there actions individuals could be taking to speed their personal adjustment to change?
- What are the special responsibilities of management in helping the team adapt to these changes?

Step 4: Implementing Change: The Issues List

- Ask the team to list those changes that are in need of immediate action because of their current impact on the team.

- Prioritize the items.
- Return to the Issues List, add any new issues needing action, and create the appropriate action items to deal with them.

MAKING IT PERMANENT

—

If you have successfully formed your Vision Statement, cascaded it throughout the organization, increased participation, and survived the often difficult changes required—you've made a great start.

Your job isn't over, though.

You are through with Stage 2 of the change–effort curve, but there is still more to do. You must now make those cultural changes permanent. Your task now is to translate the concepts of your Vision Statement into the constant and durable systems you use to run your business. Only when the vision becomes systemic will it become permanent. One of management's primary roles in the new organization will be to establish and sustain these systems.

The chapters in this section deal with how to build these systems so that the changes you have made to implement vision and increase participation become permanent.

12

CONTINUOUS CULTURAL IMPROVEMENT (CCI)

This chapter discusses something that for many managers will be a new concept: building a process whereby leadership takes on the commitment to continuously improve the culture of the organization.

In the new organization, it is management's role to create a safe environment where people's creativity can flourish. In this culture of trust and participation, the organization of the future begins to take shape. Ideas begin to percolate, innovation and creativity are the norm, and it becomes safe to take risks. Problem solving and communication are greatly increased. All of these things act to accelerate organizational velocity.

By empowering the front line, you are asking them to become accountable for the continuous improvement of the operations and systems of the organization. In return, leadership must reciprocate by becoming accountable for the continuous improvement of the culture.

Once this reciprocal agreement between management and staff is reached, managers are left with one substantial question. How do you account for—or measure—continuous cultural improvement?

MEASURING THE GOOSE

In the past, American business has been preoccupied with measuring only the golden egg—its annual profits. The goose that laid the egg has been ignored. The result has been a loss of standing in worldwide markets. To regain that velocity, we must build accounting systems for the *people* whose creative talents produce those financial results. As important as it is to measure financial performance, it is equally important to regularly measure the health of the work culture.

Continuous improvement must occur not only in the manufacturing or service delivery systems, but in the most important place of all: the culture of the people who do the work. This is where you will put your vision into action—permanently. Cultural improvement must figure prominently in all management planning. *Give the same emphasis to cultural issues you give to financial issues.*

You Get What You Measure

Building and improving your organization's culture begins with measuring how well you are translating your vision into action. Specifically, you must assure that the culture is growing in a way that is consistent with the organization's Mission Statement and Guiding Principles.

Without a system of measurement, you have no reliable way of knowing the health and vitality of the culture. Once you build such a system, though, you can begin to collect the data that will help you measure cultural improvement—much as you now measure your financial improvement.

Measure the Right Things

Historically, companies have used incentives primarily to recognize financial performance. Organizations must now begin to measure and reward those actions that help turn each organization's unique vision—its Mission and Guiding Principles—into reality. These measurements should occur two or three times a year.

Companies must begin to measure such things as:

Vision

Teamwork

Quality of communication

Coaching

Trust in management

Empowerment

Risk taking and innovation

Fairness of reward and recognition

Leadership

Cooperation among teams

Problem solving

Commitment to quality

Integrity

Use the Results

These cultural measurements will yield results only if you follow through with action plans. Once you understand the relative health of the work culture, plan to use the information to make immediate improvements.

Continuous improvement is just that: continuous. It is a journey, not a destination. Managers should never feel satisfied with the culture and forget about it. For managers and employees of the new organization, continuous improvement—making the vision a reality—is a career-long commitment.

CCI begins largely with an observation of trends. When the trends are positive, managers should determine the reasons and strive to make them permanent. When the culture shows signs of stress, the problems should be immediately identified and solved.

Leadership through CCI builds trust and participation. When managers translate their mission and values into numbers available to the organization, they demonstrate their willingness to be held accountable. The process also illustrates the managers' commitment to the mission and values of the company. These actions quickly build trust in the company and make it safer for people to participate in the organization.

CCI LEADERSHIP SKILLS

Most senior management teams bring a great deal of skill and insight into the examination of their financial results. As they study profit-and-loss statements and other financial details, they ask questions, probe deeply, and don't stop until they understand why profits have dropped or why margins are shrinking in a certain market. They know that it takes perseverance and stamina to become skillful financial planners. These same executives, however, have usually developed only superficial skills for managing their culture. They spend far less time—if any—on cultural improvement.

In the new organization, continuous cultural improvement is a process that will occupy much of every manager's day. It initially requires creating a flow of data. It is only through scrutinizing the data with the same vigor and attentiveness they apply to financial data that any manager can become skilled at CCI.

Learning this skill is not just an option, it is a necessity. The ability to understand, measure, and maintain CCI will have a profound impact on an organization's competitiveness—and ultimately on its very survival.

It is important to realize that developing this skill takes time—usually as much or more time than developing the financial skills required for the job. Acquiring a depth of understanding about the organizational culture, then designing methods to continuously improve it, will require relentless effort. It won't happen overnight, but for those who take the trouble, continuous cultural improvement is an obtainable goal.

Striking a Balance

CCI provides a methodology that builds participation, trains people in problem solving, and invites leadership. It is a process that creates a balance in the organization between financial concerns and cultural concerns. It also strikes a balance between continuous quality improvement in the manufacturing and service end of the organization and continuous cultural improvement on the people side.

Avoiding the Pitfalls

Some companies have worked at building a method of measuring their culture, yet have fallen behind because they have not generated reliable data. Still others have misfired by not improving their organization's problem-solving ability. In addition, by not encouraging employee participation in improving the work culture, organizations fail to fully embed continuous improvement in the management systems of the organization.

Measuring Your Vision

Begin to measure the work culture by first focusing on elements of your organization's vision: the Mission and accompanying Glossary in addition to the Guiding

Principles you have led the company in developing. You must build a cultural survey to measure these unique characteristics of your vision. By initially focusing your attention on these items, you will collect the data necessary to judge how well you are succeeding in building a culture based on leadership, trust, and participation.

CHOOSING THE BEST STUDY.   Basically, you have a choice between a traditional study and a causal study. We strongly recommend you choose a causal study. In a traditional study, management compiles a list of the questions it would like to ask the employees. Most issues are addressed with a single question (for example, "How satisfied are you?"). The problem with this format is there is virtually no way to assess the validity of these results (did they measure what you think they measured?). It is also subject to large error because different people will interpret individual questions differently (just because of the day they have had, what someone just said to them, or what they may be angry or sad about at the moment).

A causal study does not treat individual questions as necessarily accurate in themselves. Rather, a cluster of questions (usually between five and seven) is developed for each area to be measured (such as job satisfaction). It is true that each item will contain error as in a traditional study, but when taken as a set, the items provide a clear, stable picture of what you are measuring. These, in essence, become the dots that make up a picture in a magazine. Up close, they look like just a collection of dots. From a distance, however, they take on a clear, recognizable pattern.

A traditional survey allows you only to compare data. The information you compare is broken down by division, department, job title, gender, length of service, and so on. This can be interesting, but what you end up with is a series of high and low scores. There is still no data to tell

you *which* of these high and low scores are more important, which are causes and which are effects.

A causal study becomes very interesting at this point because it asks the question "*Why* are some scores high and
others low?" It seeks to answer this question by seeing
which scores *vary together*. For example, employees who
have a high desire to quit might also report they have in-
sufficient authority to do their jobs. In a causal study, the
data analysis shows which of these areas are *causing* each
other.

With this information you begin to learn what enhances
progress in your effort to continuously improve your culture and what impedes it. It also becomes fairly apparent
where those impediments are and focuses you on just
where to spend your time and money.

Thus a causal study produces cohesive information. It
first provides high-quality, reliable data. Then it identifies
which elements of your environment are having impact on
your work culture, and finally, it shows where to concentrate time and resources in order to effectively and efficiently improve the culture.

Done consistently over time, this approach gives you an
extremely accurate picture of your organization, how it
has grown, how it has changed—and most important, *why*
these things have happened. A causal study produces the
most effective, reliable methodology for leaders to continuously improve their organization.

THE NEED FOR PROFESSIONAL SUPPORT.   Compared to a
traditional survey, a causal study is much more complex. It
involves much greater care and effort in the selection, testing, and use of questions. Where the traditional survey
ends with comparative data, the causal study is just
beginning. A professional can help to ensure the data
analysis is reliable and useful, and therefore powerful.

There are few qualified resources in the area of causal
studies. If you wish to obtain more information about

causal studies or desire assistance in identifying qualified expertise in your area, please write the authors at:

15 Central Way
Suite 194
Kirkland, WA 98033

CCI ACTION PLAN

The rest of this chapter consists of a detailed, step-by-step strategy aimed at integrating CCI into your management systems. Building CCI naturally falls into three phases.

I. **CCI measurement.** This is a periodic survey specifically designed to measure how well the methods and systems of your organization translate your vision into action.

II. **Management team action planning.** This involves the senior management team analyzing the survey data, identifying which cultural issues need to be addressed, and creating a task force to solve the problem.

III. **Task force problem solving.** This process is geared toward building participation. Task teams should be created that consist of people from all levels and departments of the organization. The teams' duties will include implementing action plans aimed at solving the problems identified by the senior management team.

CCI ACTION PLAN

I. CCI MEASUREMENT

Use a questionnaire tailored to measuring your vision to ask people for their perceptions of their work environment. You should distribute this form every four to six months. Each time you administer this survey, publicize both the results and your action plans for addressing issues you have identified.

ADMINISTERING THE QUESTIONNAIRE

This survey should be distributed to everyone in your organization. Some guidelines when administering this questionnaire:

- Ensure the confidentiality of the people who complete the survey. This can be done in a variety of ways, from providing envelopes for return, to arranging for collection boxes throughout the office.
- Do not allow more than a week for people to complete and return the questionnaire. It will only get lost in the shuffle. A survey can be completed in 10 to 15 minutes, so you may choose to have them filled out at a staff meeting.

It is important to ensure that all employees understand the purpose of the survey and how you will use the results. For this reason, include an explanatory memo with each administration of the questionnaire.

II. MANAGEMENT TEAM ACTION PLANNING

GOALS

- Make a priority list of your most critical issues.
- Assign those issues to cross-functional teams.

PROCESS OVERVIEW

1. Rank the critical issues.
2. Assign issues to task teams drawn from throughout the organization.
3. Publicize assessment data and plans for resolution.

STEP 1: IDENTIFY THE CRITICAL ISSUES

Having read the survey data, use the following matrix to rank the importance of any problems indicated by your results. For each area of measurement, record the average and the trend (a percentage up or down). With these results in mind, indicate whether you believe this to be a serious issue. Compare the scores to determine which issues need your attention.

Areas of Measurement	Average/ Trend	**IMPACT** (1 = Not an issue; 10 = Serious issue)						
		Em- ployees	Cus- tomers	Cost	Profits	Quality	Total	Rank
Goals & values	/							
Teamwork	/							
Job satisfaction	/							
Stress	/							
Prob. solving	/							
Risk/ideas	/							
Empowerment	/							
Role	/							
Communication	/							
Service quality	/							

(This is just a sample template—be sure these areas reflect your priorities.)

The areas with the highest scores are the most important to work on. Select two or three critical issues. Initially, it is best to concentrate on just a few. The number can increase with your organization's ability to solve problems.

STEP 2: SELECT TASK TEAM

A manager on the team should assume responsibility for each critical issue. This person's role is that of "center-post," overseeing the process rather than directly leading it. The procedure is as follows:

- Select five to seven individuals from across the organization to form a task team. The team's challenge will

be to reduce or resolve the problem it is presented
with.

- The manager is accountable for ensuring the team
  has effective leadership and is productive, *without* directly assuming the role of leader.

- The manager will be a liaison to the rest of the management team as solutions are devised and acted
  upon. This is for the purpose of obtaining any necessary support from the management team as the manager paves the way for his or her task team to do its job
  and prepare to implement the action plan that they
  will develop.

STEP 3: PUBLICIZE CCI MEASUREMENT AND PLANS FOR IMPROVEMENT

Talk to your staff about the results of the latest measurement. Tell them which areas of cultural health have been
designated as critical issues. Each employee should receive
the following:

- A copy of the latest survey results.
- A cover letter explaining the work of the management
  team including:
  (a) listing of new critical issues
  (b) members of each cross-functional task team as-
      signed to address the issues
  (c) summary and celebration of the previous task
      teams' results

Do not merely distribute the report. Rather, have each department and/or work unit make it the topic of discussion
in their next meeting. *In order to succeed, CCI must be discussed and publicized.* Consider having a management team
member present in as many of these meetings as
possible.

III. TASK FORCE PROBLEM SOLVING

GOAL

- Substantially reduce or eliminate the impact of a critical issue to your organization.

PROCESS OVERVIEW

1. Form the team.
2. Describe the issue.
3. Determine the causes.
4. Develop a solution.
5. Create the action plan.
6. Put the plan into action.
7. Follow up.

STEP 1: FORM THE TEAM

- Elect a team leader. The management team member is not eligible for this role. Responsibilities of the team leader include:

Keeping the team focused on its goal.

Making sure everyone contributes and no one person dominates.

Facilitating a thorough discussion of all facets of the issue.

Maintaining an efficient pace.

Monitoring implementation of the action plan that your team will produce.

- Elect a secretary. Responsibilities of the secretary include:

  Summarizing the discussions and decisions of the team and distributing to all members.

  Summarizing the action plan and distributing it to all team members.

- The role of the management team member is to be a *resource* to the task team from the management level. Attend all meetings and act to remove any outside barriers to the successful functioning of the task team. The management team member will bring to bear any resources that are required for the task team to accomplish its mission. In addition, the manager is accountable to the management team for the team's success.

- Make sure that everyone is focused on the *purpose* of the task team. To do this, briefly develop a Mission

---

EXAMPLE

Mission Statement

To increase teamwork throughout our company by understanding the causes of poor teamwork, developing positive solutions, and implementing them in an effective manner.

Guiding Principles

We treat each other with trust and respect.
We keep our promises to each other.
We demand of ourselves the highest integrity in our dealings with each other.
We listen to each other without defensiveness.
We promptly and responsibly raise and resolve issues that interfere with our work or our relationships.

Statement with the team. Consider these questions: Who are we? What will we do? For whom? Why? In addition, it will be helpful to create the team's guiding principles: those values that will serve as the foundation for the team members' relationships with one another and the rest of your organization.

STEP 2: DESCRIBE THE ISSUE

Carefully examine your critical issue by listing the symptoms of the issue. Look closely at any results, conditions, or events that indicate there is a problem.

EXAMPLE

Description of the Issue

Issue: Judging from our latest CCI results, the teamwork in our company appears to be on the *decrease*. The trend is significantly down over the last two surveys.

Symptom 1: The managers of the Credit and Customer Service departments are not speaking to each other.

Symptom 2: The Sales department is up in arms about not getting enough support from the Marketing, Customer Service, or Credit departments. Sales people are threatening to leave.

Symptom 3: We have lost a lot of customers lately.

Issue Description: Customer service is suffering because the Marketing, Credit, and Customer Service departments are not coordinating their efforts, communications have broken down, and conflicts exist among them.

Avoid letting this become a gripe session. The job of the team is to gain a more concrete understanding of the problem to be solved.

After this examination, summarize the symptoms in a brief description. Everyone must agree on the sentence. You now have a starting point for more closely looking at, and ultimately resolving, the critical issue.

STEP 3: DETERMINE THE CAUSES

In resolving a critical issue, you must first understand its causes.

- Begin by generating a list of all possible causes of the symptoms you have described. Brainstorm possible causes using the Fishbone Diagram, a technique for visually displaying causes in several different categories. Choose categories that appear to be related to the problem. Common categories include: materials, people, physical environment, work methods, equipment, and procedures.

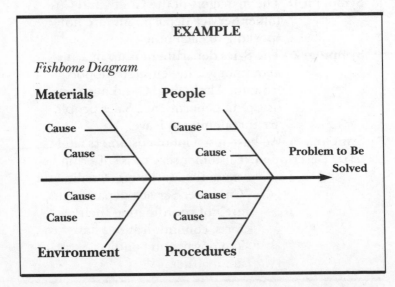

EXAMPLE

Fishbone Diagram

Materials   **People**

Cause   Cause

Cause   Cause   **Problem to Be Solved**

Cause   Cause

Cause   Cause

Environment   **Procedures**

- For each probable cause, ask what information must be gathered to verify this cause. (There will be several types of information you should consider, including numerical data, background data, and interviews with people who might have informed points of view.)
- Decide on the most likely cause or causes based on your research. Everyone must agree. You are now ready to develop a solution.

STEP 4: DEVELOP A SOLUTION

- Generate a list of potential solutions that may help in reaching the end result you desire.
- Select the criteria you will use in evaluating and choosing the solutions that will help you achieve your goal.

	IMPACT (1 = Low impact; 10 = High impact						
Potential Solutions	Employees	Customers	Cost	Profits	Quality	Total	Rank

Representative criteria can include customer satisfaction, productivity, staff retention, operating costs, time, quality improvement, and others.

- Using a matrix such as the one on page 199, rank the potential solutions and select those that will most likely enable you to resolve the problem.

STEP 5: CREATE AN ACTION PLAN

A solution requires not only an approach to solving your problem, but also a step-by-step plan that includes dates and individual responsibilities. Here is what you must do:

- List and number all action steps in sequential order.
- Determine who must be contacted and/or worked with outside the team itself.
- Determine beginning and ending dates for each step.
- Determine final completion date.
- Determine who is responsible for each step.

STEP 6: PUT THE PLAN INTO ACTION

It is time for the task team to make its work known to the management team.

- Set a meeting with the management team to present an overview of the task team's work involving the problem, its causes, proposed solution, and action plan. The purpose of this meeting is for the management team to ratify the action plan and provide whatever resources are necessary in order to reduce or eliminate the impact of the critical issue on your organization.

- Once the plan is ratified by the management team, it is time for the manager who has been acting as "centerpost" for this issue to drive the implementation of the action plan organization-wide marshaling the resources of your organization to ensure a successful final result. Follow the plan carefully. Work to meet or exceed the completion dates that have been established.

STEP 7: FOLLOW UP

Meet with the management team at least monthly to keep them informed of progress. At the same time, the rest of the organization will want to know of your progress as well.

- Consider a joint communication from both the management and task teams each month until the team's goal has been reached.

- Remember that actual progress will be charted every six to twelve months, as another CCI Measurement is taken.

13

BUILDING THE SYSTEMS

If the internal systems of your organization are still geared to supporting a hierarchical structure, your efforts toward a new organization have the future of the Ford Edsel.

As the old top-down structure is dismantled, internal systems must be changed to reflect and support the newly established Mission and Guiding Principles of the company. They must support the empowered and participative culture of the new organization.

As we mentioned earlier, the exact forms these new systems will take haven't yet been determined. Self-managed teams, quality improvement teams, and other organizational forms are being explored, and combinations of these efforts are being developed.

Whatever the forms you finally choose for your organization, the new systems must have one overriding purpose: to make your vision permanent.

No vision can be achieved simply through the strength of will of a leader. While the new leader must be an

effective and persuasive communicator, wearing the values
and mission of the organization on his or her sleeve, those
efforts will not be enough to make the vision permanent.
To weave the vision into the fabric of the organization, you
must make it a common thread throughout all the systems
that influence how people behave toward each other and
toward the customer.

Leaders must take a long, hard look at all the internal
systems to determine how they can be modified or re-
structured to support the new organization. Moving toward the new organization means changing these systems
as much as changing people's mind-sets regarding the
hierarchy.

This is a job that must be done carefully and thoroughly.
There is always the danger that any one of the systems in
the organization, if left unchanged, can defeat the vision.

It is important that leaders understand the danger that
lurks here. The action your organization takes will speak
louder than management's words. If even one system
pushes people in the direction of the old hierarchy, it can
wreck the months of work you have just completed. Over
the course of time, your organization will be defined by
its systems.

This chapter analyzes some of the primary organizational and management systems that must be changed in
order to support the Mission and Guiding Principles of
the company. At the same time, these systems must also
support, rather than hinder, all aspects of your organization in order to realize your vision.

HIRING, PROMOTING, FIRING

The systems you establish to handle these three personnel decisions are critical to making vision permanent. As
you talk about values and attempt to make them the reality

in your organization, what you *do* will be far more important than what you say. Who you hire, promote, relocate, and fire will send a powerful message throughout your organization.

Hiring

An effective vision is exclusionary. Not everyone will understand the vision; even fewer can embrace it. Those who do, however, are likely to be the exceptional people that an organization needs to become a winner.

As soon as you are clear about the kind of person the organization needs, changing how you hire need not wait. Look to your Guiding Principles. Will the individuals you are considering as employees be able to live up to those principles? Given your vision of customer service, are they the best choice to serve your customers? Beyond technical abilities, what type of interpersonal skills do they possess? Will they be a creative and participative addition to the work teams? Will they support and add to a fear-free, creative internal culture?

When hiring managers, determine whether they are capable of building culture and possess strong communication skills. These are abilities that have not been universally required of most managers in the past.

Increasingly, the hiring of staff members is being left to the teams that would include the new worker. As teams are becoming increasingly self-managing, they are given responsibility to determine who will work with them.

Vision determines hiring practices in two ways. First, it allows the organization to calibrate its expectations regarding new employees. It helps define the type of person the organization needs as it moves forward.

Second, those doing the hiring can immediately introduce the candidate to the vision of the organization. This exposes the candidate directly to the Mission and

Guiding Principles and makes clear what will be expected of him or her. During that first interview, those doing the hiring can talk about customer service, product quality, the need for teamwork, and the importance of culture.

Promoting

Who you promote speaks eloquently of your values. Promoting those who are creative problem solvers and act according to the Mission and Guiding Principles sends a forceful message throughout the organization. Conversely, promoting someone who acts in a way inconsistent with the Mission and Guiding Principles makes a liar out of you and a failure out of your attempt to implement your vision.

A useful exercise for any management team is to identify the characteristics and skills necessary for a manager to be effective. Next, the team should identify steps to take to ensure that those who are promoted or hired into the management team possess those abilities.

Reassigning, Firing

This is a topic we discuss with reluctance because it goes against the grain of building trust and participation. There may be times, however, when you must face a painful personnel decision. In making the change to the new organization, you have changed the standards for evaluating people's success. You have changed the yardstick used to measure management and frontline effectiveness. Though most people rise to the occasion and find new ways to succeed in the new organization, there may be some for whom all your attempts to empower and inspire them will fail. It becomes a question of fit. It is not a personal judgment—no one is right or wrong—it is simply a question of whether the individual fits into the new organization.

Termination is never an easy task, but the cost to the organization of not dealing with an individual whose actions are contrary to the Mission and Guiding Principles is high. The presence of this person will continually undermine everything you and the team have tried to establish. It leaves management open to charges of hypocrisy and may damage the precious trust you have worked so hard to build.

If you have someone on your team who is performing contrary to the Mission and Guiding Principles, you must take action. In many cases this action, as personally uncomfortable as it might be, is the most convincing thing you can do to show your commitment to the organizational values.

Rather than terminating, you may be able to relocate problem employees to positions where their contact with other people is minimized. This flies in the face of conventional wisdom, for example, that says no one can survive being moved from a management to a nonmanagement role. Yet in an organization that places increasing importance on nonmanagement roles, it looks less like a demotion than it has in the past.

Recently we worked with a large financial services company that had decided to make the change into a flattened organization with more participation and a limited hierarchy. One of the managers, who had been with the company for some time, was a brilliant technician. He was perhaps the most knowledgeable person in the company about certain transactions and often handled the technical side of large financial deals. However, he was an irascible curmudgeon who could not get along with other people. The company spent a considerable amount of money and time trying to help him develop leadership skills. The effort failed. It was evident that he was not a

natural leader and never would be. But, his knowledge
and experience were too valuable to lose.

The CEO solved the problem by taking him out of the
team environment and placing him where he could still
make his technical contributions without poisoning the
harmonious culture the CEO was trying hard to establish.
It worked for the organization and for the individual. After
the initial shock of the move passed, the manager found
he liked his new position better than his old one. He
didn't have to work with people and could remain where
he was comfortable—in a world of facts and figures. Termination, in this case, would have been the wrong choice.
The manager would have lost his job and the company
would have lost his valuable skills.

PERFORMANCE APPRAISAL

Performance appraisal has long been a controversial
system, even within the hierarchy. The debate over performance appraisal continues in the new organization.
W. Edwards Deming insists companies should abolish performance appraisal, claiming it robs the frontline teams of
the "ownership" of what they do.

In this case, however, we do not agree with him. Perhaps
in an ideal world, abolishing performance appraisal might
work. But in the real world, there are four reasons it is still
necessary.

First, without it, employers would face great exposure
under employment-at-will laws. There are a number of
people in protected categories involving tenure, gender,
and minority status who (for good reason) are given support in an attempt to remedy past discriminatory employ-
ment decisions. Operating without performance appraisal
data leaves a company virtually defenseless in the event of
an accusation that the company has been discriminatory

in its actions. The company cannot defend itself in its assertion that it has acted in an objective manner.

Second, without performance appraisal, it is difficult to hold people individually accountable. There will be times in the new organization when a team might achieve high marks even though one or two individuals were not contributing. Performance appraisal provides a way to evaluate team members as well as the team itself.

Third, performance appraisal is important as a tool to determine promotions.

Finally, everyone can benefit from constructive feedback about strengths and areas needing improvement. Performance appraisal, at its best, should represent effective coaching, mentoring, and teaching. It should be considered a valuable resource that helps individuals grow and stay on track in their development.

Building an effective system of performance appraisal isn't always easy. If the appraisal process doesn't feel constructive, it will probably do more harm than good. Efforts should be directed at making this process effective. To borrow an adage from a few years ago: "If it feels good, do it." If it doesn't, however, change your method to make sure that it is a positive and helpful exercise for individuals, rather than a painful or negative experience that undermines morale.

One of the reasons this process has been controversial in the past is that it has been strongly identified with the old hierarchical method of management. Consider the activity. A boss sits down with a subordinate and says, "Here is your job description." At the end of an allotted time, they sit down again and the boss says, "Here's how I think you did." Totally dictatorial in nature, as a system it has been one of the pillars of the old structure.

In the new organization, such performance appraisals by the boss are far less relevant. The boss's appraisal is too often just the hierarchy talking. In many cases, a boss doesn't know how well the employee is doing. What is often taking its place is the far more effective approach of performance appraisals done by peers. Self-managed teams are assuming this responsibility, without the need for the hierarchy to intervene. This requires a great deal of training, however. Not everyone is able to coach and give constructive feedback. Most people are likely to think of performance appraisals in terms of the ones they have experienced in more hierarchical organizations.

Many of today's organizations are moving toward a system of performance appraisals using information from a combination of five sources. A single employee will receive appraisals from peers, internal customers, staff (if a manager), self, and (last and least) the boss. Feedback from this combination can add up to one appraisal. It is effective because it reflects the entire range of a person's work.

Just as vision should be a part of your hiring process, it should play a major role in the appraisal process as well. Those making the appraisal should look to determine how well the subject is performing in accordance with the Mission and Guiding Principles. For example, the appraisal should center on how well the person participates and operates as a team player and extends himself or herself to reach the team's goals.

Organization leaders should take time to ensure that the performance appraisal system be modified to reflect these changes. A system that is still tied to the old values of the hierarchy will act as an anchor slowing the organizational changes you have worked so hard to accomplish.

SALARY AND INCENTIVES

Salary has traditionally been a major tool of the hierarchy. Salary and moving up in the hierarchy have always been bound together in lockstep. But in the new organization, salary is no longer based on seniority and rank as it has been in the past. In the new organization, salary will be used to encourage a totally different set of accomplishments. Rather than being based on seniority and rank, salary is increasingly being based on skills and accomplishment.

As work teams become increasingly cross-functional, taking on a broader variety of tasks, missions, and goals, team members must possess a wide range of skills. Team members become more valuable to the team according to their versatility and attitude. In the new organization, salaries are based on the mastery of these attributes and not on "moving up." This approach to salary provides an incentive to people to grow in their professional abilities.

In addition to salary, an increasing portion of take-home pay is being provided in the form of incentives and bonuses. The shift here is to team-based incentives rather than individual rewards. This leads to a focus on teamwork and collaboration, rather than the success of individual efforts. The form this often takes is gain sharing for quality improvements. When a team comes up with a method of quality improvement that saves money, a certain percentage of the savings is shared by the team. The interdependence that team incentives create motivates the team members to help increase one another's performance, through constructive performance appraisals and other methods.

CAREER PATHS

The college graduating class of 1990, when asked what they felt was the most important element when choosing a new job, answered: "The opportunity to move up the ladder."

It's clear that they don't yet get the joke. The irony of this answer is that they are about to enter a business environment where the ladder will soon have far fewer rungs. To paraphrase Gertrude Stein, "There is no 'up' there." In the new organization, with its drastically reduced layers of hierarchy, "upward mobility" will no longer be relevant. What will take its place will be "horizontal fast tracks" that management must create. These fast tracks will provide opportunities for employees to grow, and to expand their skills, responsibilities, and paychecks. If the fast tracks are established correctly, employees will achieve by collaborating rather than by clawing their way to the top.

In the old hierarchical organization, people were motivated by and put their creative energies only into getting their next promotion. Their entire focus was on moving up. The whole idea of increasing personal skills and achieving personal vision was overshadowed by the competitive scramble up the corporate ladder. This all changes in the new organization. With the hierarchy dismantled and salaries being tied to skills rather than rank, career paths will become much more horizontal.

RECOGNITION

Recognition is a basic human need and one of the key elements of job satisfaction. A recent national poll revealed that two-thirds of American workers would, all other factors being equal, willingly move to another company where employee recognition was a high priority. In other words, they did not feel their own company valued them, because their work was not recognized. In most companies, this is not so much the fault of individual managers as it is the lack of an effective *system* of acknowledgment.

Management often fails to understand how crucial these systems are to a healthy work culture and an inspired work force. While many managers understand this on an intellectual level and may harbor good intentions, few do anything about it in a meaningful way. *As a result, lack of recognition of employees' efforts has become one of the biggest failings of American management.*

In the new organization, recognition systems must become permanent. This is especially important for companies undergoing a change to increase participation and empowerment. Employees must receive recognition whenever they demonstrate success at implementing the Guiding Principles and the Mission. It is equally important to acknowledge their increased teamwork abilities. Although this type of recognition does not have to include financial rewards and can be done in an informal manner, it is still essential to the success of the company.

One of the more intriguing systems of recognition was created a few years ago by the Paul Revere Insurance Corporation. It is called the PEET Plan (Process for Ensuring that Everyone is Thanked). Each week, senior executives choose an individual or team that has made an exemplary contribution. The team's manager seeks out the winners at their workplace during the workday and publicly thanks them for their efforts. The system is highly popular with the employees, who see it as a clear example that management means what it says about recognizing extraordinary effort.

NEW EMPLOYEE ORIENTATION

Traditionally, new employee orientation has included tours of the facilities, introductions to employee benefits, and the like. In the new organization, orientation is also seen as an opportunity to introduce vision and culture to the new employee. This includes a cascading-like discussion of the company's Mission and Guiding Principles and management's pledge to maintain a fear-free culture. This type of values clarification is extremely useful as a systematic part of the orientation program.

TRAINING

Training is the primary method of equipping the front line with the ability and skills to accept greater responsibility. The process of empowering the front line usually will not work unless employees are prepared through proper training. Untrained employees often become confused and frustrated by their new responsibilities, and decision making comes to a halt.

Frontline people aren't the only ones who need training. Managers must also learn how to become culture builders and leaders. Many companies in the United States and in Japan have recognized this fact. Nonhierarchical organizations spend three to four times more than traditional companies do on training.

A first step toward creating an education plan can be to identify which new skills and abilities will be required by managers and staff. Next, the plan should include the methods of teaching and communicating these skills to those who need them.

INFORMAL COMMUNICATIONS

Don't leave communication to chance. Open-door policies can't be counted on to provide the free flow of information necessary in the new organization. Continual communication must be made systemic. Recognize, though, that there is a lot more art to this than science.

One method that has been effective is the diagonal lunch. These are regularly scheduled breaks (breakfast or dinner will work as well) that are attended by a senior management representative and a number of other people chosen by drawing a diagonal line through the organizational chart. This will give people a chance to appear without their immediate supervisor, which allows them to talk directly with top management in a free flow of information and ideas. The employees are often asked to show up with at least one question. The senior manager should make sure that all the questions are answered, if not at lunch then shortly thereafter.

INFORMATION SYSTEMS

Technological systems cannot be decentralized fully, although local area networks and other computer advances are making it increasingly possible to share information company-wide. Management must ensure that work teams are given as much information as quickly as possible. This is especially important as the teams become self-managing. As they take on more of the traditional decision-making roles of management, they will need all the information once reserved for their bosses.

Information systems must become a part of the empowering process in the new organization. Management must purchase data systems that can get information to the work teams quickly and efficiently. In many companies this will mean that management should take the control of the information flow out of the hands of the Information Systems department and route it directly to the work teams by way of PC or mini-networks. In companies where computer-generated information is not of direct importance to the front line, managers must still determine what information the work teams require and get it to them as quickly as possible.

CONTINUOUS QUALITY IMPROVEMENT

CQI systems can take many forms. However you structure
your system, make sure that it includes an ongoing process
that involves every person working with others in some way
to improve work methods. These systems include quality
improvement teams trained to use "the quality sciences."
These are tools for identifying problems in work methods
and developing solutions to these problems. The goal of
the CQI efforts should be to move closer to the ideal of
meeting customer expectations 100 percent of the time
with zero waste or mistakes.

NO OVERNIGHT CHANGES

We include this sample list of systems knowing that there is
no single form these systems will take. The prototypes are
only now being built. Every manager must find what works
best for his or her company.

There may be a number of ways to conduct a performance appraisal, give incentives, recognize employees, or
provide the needed training; the form itself is not our concern here. What matters is that the systems you create further the goals of your Vision Statement. These systems
should act to translate the effort you have put into creating
the Vision Statement, cascading it, and managing the
change into an enduring process. They should act to make
your vision permanent.

The new organization should not require the strength
of will of any single person to succeed. Your vision and
the systems that support it must be robust enough to survive you or any other individual in the company. This will
happen if these systems are embedded in every aspect of
the organization.

Transforming all your management systems is not a simple task, and it won't happen overnight. It is a long-term process. Have patience. In fact, use caution, lest these changes occur *too* fast. Quick, massive changes may overwhelm people's capacity to absorb them. Managers must have a feel for how fast they can implement these changes—then they should do so at the highest rate of speed the organization can handle.

14

STAYING IN ACTION

Blazing the trail as a visionary leader is not for the meek or fainthearted. Choosing to be a leader who exerts influence by empowering others, rather than through direct control, is a major-league decision. Far more than a management tool, it is a philosophy of life that defines your interactions and relationships with other people. (It has the potential to transcend the workplace, but in this book we contain our thoughts to that arena.)

However far you decide to take this philosophy, one thing is essential: You must make a permanent commitment to it. Through the Vision Statement, you have made certain promises and have asked for your staff's trust in return. In essence, you have made a sacred pact with each other and neither of you can break it without great damage to your organization. Your end of the bargain will be fulfilled only if you remain committed to the principles that drive the new vision. In that regard, the journey never ends. There are numerous rewards along the way, but the effort itself is continuous. You can never stop doing what you need to do to nourish the bonds of trust you have established.

DEVELOP YOUR INSTINCTS

As a new leader, you will be more like an athlete than a scientist. Events will often swirl around you at great speed and you must be ready to react immediately to them. Periodically you may have the luxury of time to make a carefully calculated decision, but that is likely to be the exception rather than the rule. Often there will be no set management script to follow. When the game is on, you must be able to anticipate, react, and trust your instincts to make the right decision.

The most successful leaders are those who work relentlessly at recognizing and seizing leadership opportunities. Like "crunch time" in a ball game, these are crucial moments when you must make important decisions. For the new leader, these manifest themselves in opportunities to teach and inspire people, and communicate values and purpose. Your performance during these crunch times will mean as much or more to your team or organization as Michael Jordan's or Wayne Gretzky's performances have been to theirs.

Constant Renewal

Like those extraordinary athletes, you must stay in shape as a leader. While you may not have to do a 360-degree slam dunk, you do have to constantly exercise your leadership abilities. This means putting yourself into situations where your sensibilities are sharpened, your values are challenged and clarified, and where you are pushed to the limit in your ability to lead.

To give you an idea of what we mean, we have selected 10 exercises that will help keep your leadership abilities well honed.

1. *Write a personal Vision Statement.* Just as your organization needs an articulated mission and set of guiding

principles to stay on track, so do you. Take ample time to develop this personal Vision Statement, which should consist of a Mission Statement and Guiding Principles.

In thinking about your Mission Statement, consider how you express yourself through your work. How do you find satisfaction there? In what ways are you of service to others? The opportunity here is to find self-expression and meaning in the work you are doing. In thinking through your personal mission, consider the same questions you asked when writing the team's Mission Statement. Who are you? What do you do? For whom? Why?

A health-care executive we have worked with gave us permission to use the Mission Statement he developed as a way to clarify his personal values.

"I am a health-care leader dedicated to enabling my patients to live long and healthy lives; and to supporting my staff in finding self-expression and satisfaction in their professional lives." He told us that checking his Mission Statement every few months has helped him stay in close touch with those values.

Next, develop personal Guiding Principles. Take some time to reflect on which values guide your actions as a leader and which drive your relationships with other people. Think about how these values translate into actions. We recommend that you write the answers down and evaluate them from time to time. For example, our health-care executive wrote:

"I will always strive to expand my professional knowledge; spare no effort in helping my staff develop themselves; recognize their contributions; and most important, continue to strive to deliver the best possible health care for my patients."

In developing your personal Vision Statement, it is important to use your organization's Vision Statement as a starting point. There should be no inconsistencies between the two.

2. *Review both Vision Statements regularly.* At least twice a
   year, you and your team or organization should examine the organizational Vision Statement to ensure
   it is still relevant to what you and the organization are
   doing. Have any changes occurred in the organization that require a revision? Are there any new services, customers, or standards not encompassed by
   the Vision Statement? Have any incidents over the
   past few months suggested a need for changes or ad-
   ditions? The review of the organization's Vision Statement is also a good time to review your own.

3. *Clarify your leadership philosophy.* The best business
   leaders are philosophers who examine the human
   condition and the role of work in people's lives. They
   probe motivations and ask what people need to stay
   inspired and creative and to fulfill themselves at the
   highest level. They see leadership as an opportunity
   to contribute to the quality of the lives of those they
   lead.

   Devote time to articulate your own philosophy of
   leadership: your assumptions, values, commitments,
   and hopes. Consider some of the following questions:

   • What is my responsibility to my staff?
   • What are my most important roles?
   • What do people need from me?
   • What do people want from me?

   When answering these questions, focus on the contributions you want to make to others in your role as
   a leader and the principles that will guide your actions. Make sure you give this exercise the time it
   needs.

4. *Always be teaching.* Find people to mentor. Teach
   them how to communicate, lead, and accept empowerment. This will have a twofold benefit. It makes

your employees more productive and it keeps you in touch with the values you espouse in your personal Vision Statement. Get to know those you mentor. This includes listening to their hopes and career aspirations. Devote time to helping them develop career plans and listening to how they feel about their work.

5. *Create a peer group.* As a leader, you'll find feedback from your peers can be extremely helpful. If there is no such group available, be active in putting one together, either from your organization or from the professional community around you. The effort will be worth it. You can learn a great deal from one another by sharing philosophies of leadership as well as discussing the realities of the job—what works and what doesn't. And don't hesitate to be mentored yourself. If there is a leader in your organization or community you particularly admire, spend time with him or her and learn whatever you can.

6. *Know yourself.* Identify the gaps between where you are as a leader and where you want to be. Ask for honest feedback from your peers and staff. Ask them for suggestions on changes you can make to be more effective. Be sure that if you ask, you listen to their answers. Any defensiveness on your part will shut down the communication. Your openness to constructive ideas serves as an example and encourages others to react similarly when given improvement suggestions.

7. *Create your own personal development plans.* Act on the feedback you receive. The biggest obstacle to this will be your other responsibilities. It's easy to push self-improvement down the priority list until it gets lost. Don't allow this to happen. Instead, you must make continual self-improvement a lifelong challenge. Attend seminars, talk with peers and consultants, and

read books and journals that challenge your ideas. Keep thinking, keep growing.

8. *Manage your calendar.* Don't let the pull of the technical side of your work keep you from staying in close communication with your team. Each week, schedule time for walking the halls and talking with people, meeting one-on-one with those who need it and giving airtime to the Vision Statement. If someone can't tell from your calendar that you are a leader, you aren't a leader. Make sure your goals and relationships get the time they deserve.

9. *Always have big projects in action.* Whether it is opening up a whole new market, restructuring your company, starting self-managed teams, establishing continuous quality improvement systems, or any other major change, strive to have at least one major project under way. If you aren't involved with a project that requires the full extent of your leadership abilities, you aren't asking enough of yourself or your team.

10. *Always be in the Middle Zone of some major change.* The Middle Zone, of course, is that time of confusion between the ending of an old system and the beginning of a new one. As you move through a variety of changes and become accustomed to life in the Middle Zone, it will lose its ferocious appearance. If you are not confused about something important, you are not changing enough. Being constantly in the Middle Zone of one major change or another means you will always be testing and expanding your beliefs and practices.

CREATE A COVENANT WITH YOUR COMPANY

Your relationship with your organization is one filled with promise and obligation. As you ask people to commit themselves intellectually and emotionally to the purpose and values of the company, you, in exchange, must operate selflessly to provide fertile ground for their efforts. If you have done your job well, the purpose and values expressed in the Vision Statement will become important to people not only as an organizing force for business success, but in their personal lives as well.

Don't let them down.

It happens. As we mentioned earlier, some leaders can't handle the confusion of the Middle Zone and abandon the entire effort. Others, during economic crises, become authoritarian out of instinct. They fall back on the old ways, seize authority, and try to force things to happen. In doing so, they completely sabotage the trust they have built. Whatever short-term gain they may perceive, their decision in the long run will be devastating for them as leaders and for the organization. When trust is ground underfoot by an insecure or frightened leader, everyone comes out a loser.

Winners, in contrast, take a different tack. For example, one of the most successful banks in the Pacific Northwest got that way, in part, by turning the nationwide economic downturn into a benefit. The leadership made a well-publicized promise to everyone in the organization that regardless of how grim things became, no one in the bank would be laid off. In exchange, management asked for everyone's full support and participation in developing ways to improve customer service during the difficult times. The bank employees responded enthusiastically. While nearby businesses were cutting staff and regressing to top-down methods of authority, the leadership of the bank was able to strengthen its relationship with its people and improve the quality of its service.

It's important to you as a leader that you think in the long term. This is true not only with regard to your organization but also as it applies to your own motivations. Unfortunately, we have witnessed more than one leader who has done an excellent job of guiding his organization through the Vision Statement process, only to have his attention to continuous cultural improvement fade over time.

Stay in action. Maintaining your status as a world-class leader in a world-class organization requires that you remain focused on improving the sources of quality and effectiveness in your organization. That, above all else, will allow you to maintain your competitive edge.

FOLLOW A HIGHER PURPOSE

Many leaders have been power brokers looking to control and be served. Their days are numbered. In the new organization—in the new paradigm—successful leaders are driven by a higher purpose: the desire to empower and serve others.

With that in mind, it's worth asking yourself: "Am I interested in this? Does this appeal to me? Do I have what it takes to give my authority away to my staff?"

If the answer to any of these questions is no, if there is no satisfaction in this for you, don't do it. Your personal joy and fulfillment must come from giving power away, rather than wielding it like a hammer. The personal "juice" of being a visionary leader comes from the enormous satisfaction of witnessing the growth and development of those you lead. If you don't understand this—if the idea of being the boss and master of your span of control is too hard to let go of—then you should not attempt the vision process.

A DECISION OF THE HEART

After all the discussions, evaluations, and calculations are done, your decision to become a visionary leader must come from your heart. Empirically, there is ample evi-

dence from enlightened companies that empowering employees and building a participative work environment will
yield substantial productivity gains. But the new paradigm
is based on the understanding that, while profits are our
end goal, they are not our most powerful leadership focus.
In a sense, profits are analogous to breathing. We need to
breathe to live, but breathing is not the highest purpose of
our lives. Leaders need profits as a measure of success, yet
they are not the highest purpose of leading.

The irony of the role of visionary leaders is that they
must be a servant to those they lead. The paradox is that
they can lead only by giving their power away.

For those leaders who understand this and who have the
courage, stamina, and, most of all, the *vision* to share it
with others, the ultimate corollary is simple. You win, your
team wins, your company wins.

ABOUT THE AUTHORS

Robert S. Solum and **Mark R. Sobol** are the principals of **Vision In Action, Inc.**, a nationally recognized management consulting and training firm in Kirkland, Washington. Both are executive consultants, management trainers, public speakers, and authors, whose experience spans over fifteen years of consulting in a wide variety of service and manufacturing industries, including high-tech, telecommunications, information systems, transportation, aerospace, banking, insurance, and health care. They specialize in researching, developing, and implementing management systems that increase the speed and ease of organizational change.

Their unique blend of knowledge and experience in organizational design, leadership, operations, industrial psychology, and change management provides a highly practical approach to the many facets of both operational and cultural improvement. Helping businesses achieve customer satisfaction through leadership, quality, and a shared vision, Solum and Sobol are dedicated to their mission, *Helping To Change The Way America Does Business.*

Bob Wall is president of **Bob Wall and Associates,** an organizational development and training firm also located in Kirkland, Washington. Dedicated to individual and team effectiveness in the workplace, his speaking, consulting, and training focus on providing people with the tools needed for reaching their professional potential. Focusing on the cultural side of organizations, Wall has a unique capacity for enabling people to better understand and respond to the interpersonal challenges of leadership, teamwork, quality, and service. His work has reached diverse audiences across the nation, including finance, aerospace, manufacturing, transportation, health care, food marketing, and retail sales.

You can reach the authors at the following address and phone number:

15 Central Way, Suite 194
Kirkland, WA 98033
206-828-0472

INDEX